X

What is strategy
– and does it matter?

To Maria, Georgina and young Richard

What is strategy
– and does it matter?

Second Edition

Richard Whittington

THOMSON

TM

Australia • Canada • Mexico • Singapore • Spain • United Kingdom • United States

THOMSON ™

What is Strategy – and does it matter? 2nd edition

Copyright © 2001 Richard Whittington

The Thomson logo is a registered trademark used herein under licence.

For more information, contact Thomson, High Holborn House, 50-51 Bedford Row, London, WC1R 4LR or visit us on the World Wide Web at: http://www.thomsonlearning.co.uk

British Library Cataloguing-in-Publication Data
A catalogue record for this book is available from the British Library

ISBN 1-86152-377-7

First edition published by Routledge 1993
Reprinted 1994 and 1995
Reprinted by International Thomson Learning Business Press 1996, 1997 (twice), 1998 and 2000 (twice)
Second edition by Thomson Learning 2001
Reprinted 2002 by Thomson

Design and typesetting by Ferdinnand Pageworks, London
Printed in the UK by TJ International, Padstow, Cornwall

C ontents

F igures and tables

Figures

Tables

Preface

This is a strategy text with a difference. It is full of argument; it has no easy prescriptions. Before you go on, you might like a user's guide.

The book's objective is to help you think about strategy – about what to do and how to do it. Its guiding proposition is that strategy is hard. You need more than standard 'plug-and-play' techniques. Precisely to help you think seriously about strategy, this book will bombard you with different views and discrepant information. You won't be given any answers, but from what you have here and your own experience, you should finish by thinking differently. What I hope is that you will emerge with your own coherent philosophy of strategy, something that will be a resource and guide in all the unforeseeable, non-standard events and opportunities that may make up your managerial life.

The book will help you think differently in a number of ways. You will be offered four fundamentally different ways of thinking about strategy in a wide range of situations – from the challenges of leadership and change, to innovation and internationalization. These ways of thinking are first of all for you to try on and amend according to your own particular experience and circumstances. But they are also offered to remind you that not everybody may be thinking about strategy in the same way as you. As well as developing your own philosophy of strategy, you need to be clear about the philosophies of your competitors and your partners. This is all the more true in the kind of world we live in now, with such a diversity of cultural, political and social environments. To help you think about these, the book will draw on examples internationally – not just the clichés of American business, but from across Europe and Asia.

Thinking differently also means thinking in new ways. This book will expose you to some of the latest ways of thinking about strategy – from complexity theory to real options – as well as some of the current controversies – for instance, between the industry structure approach to strategy and the resource-based view. It will take examples from the new industries of the twenty first century, including e-commerce and genetic engineering. It will also draw on the new capitalist economies – the developing economies of Asia, and the transitional societies of Russia and China. In these diverse and fast-moving environments, you will be better equipped by thinking differently than by relying upon the standard prescriptions of the textbooks.

The book can be used in at least three ways. First, it is a stand-alone text. The book addresses a wide range of topics in strategic management from its various philosophical perspectives. Key dilemmas and policy alternatives are set out for each. There are many examples and pointers to further reading. Second, it can be used as a parallel text. There are plenty of good primers in strategy technique, which address the main issues in a straightforward and helpful way. The point of reading this book alongside, however, is to set the standard techniques in context and to provide something of a health warning. You should see things in the round and not trust only to orthodoxy. Third, this book can be used as a resource. The book goes deeper into the basic academic disciplines of economics and sociology than most strategy texts. It draws wider from around the world. As well as show-casing the mainstream, it also introduces insights from critical perspectives which do not take the current state of the world for granted. There are good leads here for you to follow and to take further. All can help you see further and think differently.

Thinking better and thinking differently are, ultimately, what this is all about. Good strategy rarely means doing exactly the same as everybody else.

Richard Whittington
Saïd Business School/New College
Oxford.

Acknowledgements

The author would like to thank the following: Professor Michael Hannan for granting permission to reproduce (in simplified form) Figure 2.2 on page 17; M. Gestrin, R. Knight and A. Rugman for permission to reproduce (in simplified form) Figure 2.4 on page 28; Professor Peter Temin and Oxford University Press for permission to reproduce Table 3.2 on page 47; Harcourt Inc for permission to reproduce Table 4.1 on page 64; and the OECD (Organisation for Economic Co-operation and Development) for permission to reproduce Table 7.1 on page 127.

1 What is strategy – and does it matter?

From Maine to California the capitalistic
American democrat relishes that most
American of sneers, that American Question:
'If you're so smart, why aren't you rich?'
(McCloskey 1990: 111)

Introduction

Amazon.com lists forty-seven books available with the title *Strategic Management*. Most are thick tomes, filled with charts, lists and nostrums, promising the reader the fundamentals of corporate strategy. Cursory inspection reveals that they nearly all contain the same matrices, the same authorities. There is little variety, little self-doubt. These texts generally sell at around $50.

There is a basic implausibility about these books. If the secrets of corporate strategy could be acquired for $50, then we would not pay our top managers so much. If there was really so much agreement on the fundamentals of corporate strategy, then strategic decisions would not be so hard to make. This book will not promise to make you rich, nor will it soothe you with bland unanimity. Instead it will properly treat strategy as the contested and imperfectable practice it really is. Hence the questions of the title.

Rather than taking 'strategic management' for granted, as the titles of the other texts do, this book starts from the basic question 'what is strategy anyway?' The answer matters. The four basic conceptions of strategy introduced in this book – rational, fatalistic, pragmatic and relativist – all have radically different implications for how to go about 'doing strategy'. Through the following chapters, these four basic approaches will be applied to a series of key strategic issues. In every case, the different approaches will offer you reasoned, plausible, yet fundamentally opposed prescriptions about how to act. These oppositions are often complex and hard to resolve, but what do you expect? After all, strategy isn't easy.

Profit and process in business strategy

There is not much agreement about strategy. *The Economist* (1993: 106) observes: 'the consultants and theorists jostling to advise businesses cannot even agree on the most basic of all questions: what, precisely, is a corporate strategy'. Strategy guru Michael Porter (1996) asks the question 'What is Strategy?' in the very title of an important *Harvard Business Review* article. In a recent textbook, Markides (2000: vii) admits: 'We simply do not know what strategy is or how to develop a good one'.

Instead of offering you just one kind of view, this book builds on four generic approaches to strategy.[1] The *Classical* approach, the oldest and still the most influential, relies on the rational planning methods dominant in the textbooks. Next, the *Evolutionary* approach draws on the fatalistic metaphor of biological evolution, but substitutes the discipline of the market for the law of the jungle. *Processualists* emphasize the sticky imperfect nature of all human life, pragmatically accommodating strategy to the fallible processes of both organizations and markets. Finally, the *Systemic* approach is relativistic, regarding the ends and means of strategy as inescapably linked to the cultures and powers of the local social systems in which it takes place.

The four approaches differ fundamentally along two dimensions: the *outcomes* of strategy and the *processes* by which is it made. These differences can be depicted according to the intersection of the axes in Figure 1.1. The vertical axis measures the degree to which strategy either produces profit-maximizing outcomes or deviates to allow other possibilities to intrude. The horizontal axis considers processes, reflecting how far strategies are the product of deliberate calculation or whether they emerge by accident, muddle or inertia. In short, the two axes reflect different answers to two fundamental questions: what is strategy *for*; and how is strategy *done*.

The basic assumptions of the four approaches to strategy can be read off from their positions on the two axes of Figure 1.1. Classical and Evolutionary approaches see profit maximization as the natural outcome of strategy-making; Systemic and Processual approaches are more pluralistic, envisioning other possible outcomes as well as just profit. The pairings are different with regard to processes. Here, Evolutionary approaches side with the Processualists in seeing strategy as emerging from processes governed by chance, confusion and conservatism. On the other hand, though differing over outcomes, Classical and Systemic theorists do agree that strategy can be deliberate.

The two axes are continua, of course. As we shall see, the four generic approaches contain a variety of more particular perspectives on strategy, each differently positioned along the axes. Sometimes these particular perspectives will overlap from one quadrant into another. These overlaps will be explored more fully in later chapters, but in this chapter we simply introduce the broad direction of each approach and indicate in each case some key protagonists.

Each approach has different answers for the two questions of the title. Associated with authorities such as Igor Ansoff (1965, 1991) and Michael Porter (1985, 1996), the Classical approach gives the textbook answers. Here, strategy is a rational process of deliberate calculation and analysis,

Figure 1.1 **Generic perspectives on strategy**

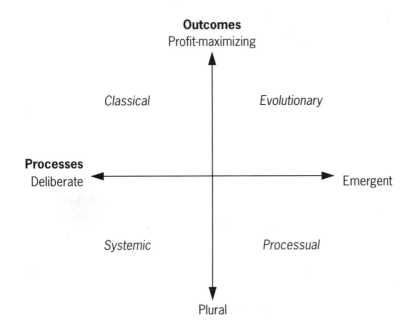

designed to maximize long-term advantage. If the effort is taken to gather the information and apply the appropriate techniques, both the outside world and the organization itself can be made predictable and plastic, shaped according to the careful plans of top management. For the Classicists, good planning is what it takes to master internal and external environments. Strategy matters in that rational analysis and objective decisions make the difference between long-run success and failure.

Evolutionists such as Hannan and Freeman (1988) or Oliver Williamson (1991) answer that strategy in the Classical sense of rational future-oriented planning is often irrelevant. The environment is typically too implacable, too unpredictable to anticipate effectively. Here the Evolutionists offer individual strategists a cruel paradox. The dynamic, hostile and competitive nature of markets means not only that long-term survival cannot be planned for; it also ensures that only those firms that somehow do hit upon profit-maximizing strategies will survive. Businesses are like the species of biological evolution: competitive processes ruthlessly select out the fittest for survival; the others are powerless to change themselves quickly enough to ward off extinction. From the Evolutionary perspective, then, it is the market, not managers, which makes the important choices. Successful strategies only emerge as the process of natural selection delivers its judgement. All managers can do is ensure that they fit as efficiently as possible to the environmental demands of the day.

Processualists agree that long-range planning is largely futile, but they are less pessimistic about the fate of businesses that do not somehow optimize environmental fit. For them, the processes of both organizations and markets are rarely perfect enough for either the strategizing of Classical theory or the survivalism of the Evolutionists. According to Cyert and March (1963), people are too different in their interests, limited in their understanding, wandering in their attention, and careless in their actions to unite around and then carry through a perfectly calculated plan. Anyway, the plan is bound to get forgotten as circumstances change. In practice, strategy emerges more from a pragmatic process of bodging, learning and compromise than from a rational series of grand leaps forward (Mintzberg 1994). It does not matter much if the emergent strategy is not quite optimal. The selection processes of the market are actually rather lax: as no-one else is likely to know what the optimal strategy is, and no-one would be able to stick to it anyway, failure to devise and carry out the perfect strategic plan is hardly going to deliver any fatal competitive disadvantage.

From the Systemic perspective, strategy does matter, but not quite in the sense that Classicists think. Systemic theorists are much less pessimistic than Processualists about people's capacity to conceive and carry out rational plans of action, and much more optimistic than Evolutionists about their ability to define their strategies in defiance of market forces. Following Granovetter's (1985) stress on the social 'embeddedness' of economic activity, the Systemic view proposes that the objectives and practices of strategy depend on the particular social system in which strategy-making takes place. Strategists often deviate from the profit-maximizing norm quite deliberately. Their social background may give them other interests than profit – professional pride, managerial power or national patriotism perhaps. The pursuit of these different objectives, even at the cost of profit maximization, is therefore perfectly rational, even if the rationale may often be disguised. Alternatively, strategists might deviate from the textbook rules of rational calculation, not because they are stupid but because, in the culture in which they work, such rules make little sense. These deviant strategies matter because they can be carried through effectively. Competitive pressures do not ensure that only Evolutionary profit-maximizers survive: markets can be manipulated or bamboozled and societies have other criteria for supporting enterprises than just financial performance. The Systemic approach, therefore, believes that strategy reflects the particular social systems in which strategists participate, defining for them the interests in which they act and the rules by which they can survive. Class and country make a difference to strategy.

Thus each perspective has its own view of strategy and how it matters for managerial practice. Classicists broadly see strategy as a rational process of long-term planning, vital to securing the future. Evolutionists usually regard the future as far too volatile and unpredictable to plan for, and warn that the best strategy is to concentrate on maximizing chances of survival today. Processualists too doubt the value of rational long-term planning, seeing strategy best as an emergent process of learning and adaptation. For both Evolutionary and Processual theorists, then, strategy in the Classical sense of rational planning does not really matter; plans are bound to be overwhelmed by events or undercut by error. Finally, Systemic theorists take a relativist position, arguing that the forms and goals of strategy-making depend particularly on social context, and that strategy should therefore be undertaken with sociological sensitivity.

The Systemic perspective also suggests that strategy matters in a different sense. Because strategies reflect the social systems in which they are enacted, firms from different systems will vary in their characteristic approaches to strategy, with potential consequences for national economic performance. In his influential *Capitalisme contre Capitalisme*, French banker and intellectual Michel Albert (1991) described an international contest between two basic forms of advanced capitalism – that of Germany, central Europe and Japan, and that of the Anglo-Saxon world, led by the United States and the United Kingdom [2]. The German/Japanese model is one of close co-operation between banks and enterprises, a paternalistic state and a communitarian view of management-worker relations. This model translates into a long-term view of strategy, a readiness to invest in equipment and training, and a respect for the hands-on skills required for technology and production. This is a view of strategy which, while not averse to planning, also values the bottom-up, incrementalism of the Processual school. On the other hand, there is the Anglo-Saxon model, associated with turbulent financial markets and impatient lenders, hostile takeovers and a hire-and-fire approach to labour. The consequences for strategy are an emphasis on short-term financial results, an aggressive external orientation to strategy, and a high valuation put on speed and flexibility. Again, this Anglo-Saxon approach does not rule out Classical planning, but it also feels very comfortable with the ruthless Evolutionary logic of 'survival of the fittest'.

These characteristic national approaches to strategy can have a big impact on national economic performance. Systemic theorists stress, however, that the influence of such characteristic strategies can change from positive to negative or from negative to positive according to the shifting demands of the economic environment. Figure 1.2 compares the growth rates in gross domestic product of Germany, Japan, the United States and the United Kingdom over the last four decades. In the early period, the German/Japanese model of strategy was generally associated with economic success: across the Pacific, the Japanese beat the United States from 1960–90, while within Europe, the Germans stayed ahead of the British until the 1980s. These periods were still dominated by the demands of large-scale mass-production of traditional goods – cars, consumer electronics, chemicals and the like. Planning ahead, but also the bottom-up contribution of committed and highly skilled workers to quality and continuous improvement, were critical in these conditions. The Anglo-Saxon economies, on the other hand, have taken off especially in the most recent period of the late 1990s, characterized by the shock of transition towards the 'new economy' of information, services, and the Internet. It looks like the fast-moving, flexible and sometimes ruthless strategizing of the Anglo-Saxon economies is better suited to the emergent economic conditions of the twenty-first century than the careful incrementalism of Germany and Japan.

The challenge of the Systemic perspective, however, is to underline the difficulties of transferring strategic philosophies and techniques from one context to another. The success of Japanese methods in the immediate post-war period, and American methods quite recently, depended upon the social systems in which they were embedded. As we have learned from the travails of Russia in the 1990s, new approaches to strategy cannot simply be grafted on. What is required, by business strategists and national policy-makers alike, is sensitivity to the kinds of strategy that are both desirable and feasible in particular times and particular places. For national policy-makers, therefore, changing characteristic strategies means change also for the social systems in which they are rooted. From the Systemic perspective, there is no easy path to optimal strategies, and recipes for success are neither universal nor timeless.

Figure 1.2 **Capitalism against capitalism: gross domestic product growth rates**

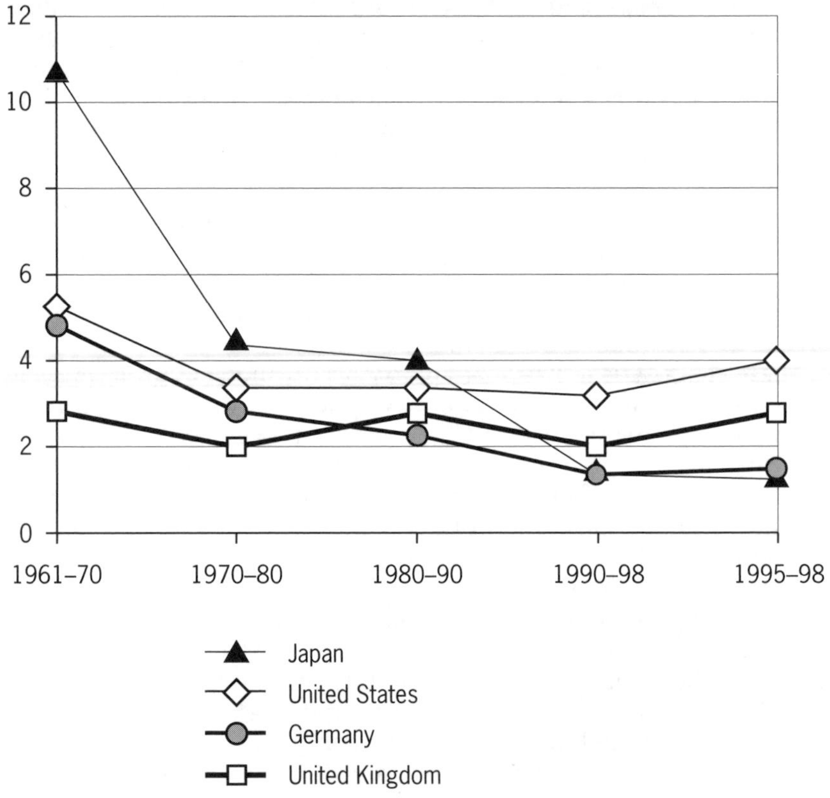

Sources: Scarpetta et al (2000); Mitchell 1976)

The plan of the book

McCloskey's (1990) 'American Question' at the start is a tough one. The theorists are not smart enough to have produced an easy rule for riches. If they had, then the rule would have been so quickly imitated that any advantage in it would have been competed away long ago. What the theorists can do, however, is point to dangers, reveal alternatives and test assumptions. In this book, then, we debate a series of key issues in strategic management from the widely differing views of the four basic approaches to strategy. On none of these issues will the debate be resolved unequivocally on one side. That is not the point. The point rather is to confront problems in all their full complexity and to recognize the diversity of means by which they can be tackled. Bogus certainties can make you poor.

The next chapter introduces the four generic approaches – Classical, Evolutionary, Processual and Systemic – in more detail. Each generic approach has very different implications for the basic ways in which you yourself should go about making strategy. The aim is therefore to make clear the context and assumptions underlying each of these four approaches so that you can test them fully against your own expectations and experience of strategy in practice.

The four middle chapters provide a chance to apply these generic approaches to central problems in strategic management. Table 1.1 outlines the sequence. Chapter 3 begins by considering who the strategists actually are, and what difference they make to strategy. Here the central debate is between the Classical protagonists of visionary leadership and Systemic theorists of both 'managerial' and 'familial' capitalism. Which argument you find most convincing will make a lot of difference to your own personal career strategies.

Table 1.1 **Issues and debates**

	Classical	Evolutionary	Processual	Systemic
Chapter 3				
Leadership	■			■
Chapter 4				
Decisions	■		□	■
Planning	■		□	□
Chapter 5				
Innovation	■		■	□
Diversification	□	■		□
Internationalization	■	■		□
Chapter 6				
Organization	■	■	□	■
Strategic change		■	■	□

Note: ■ major emphasis;
□ secondary emphasis.

Chapter 4 goes on to examine fundamental approaches to strategic choice. What value do the sophisticated techniques of finance and corporate planning have? Are they essential analytical tools, as the Classicists argue? Are they the technological props of particular professions, exercises in self-aggrandizement and legitimation, as Systemic theorists suspect? Or are they largely distractions from how strategies really get made, as the Processualists claim?

Chapter 5 looks closely at three fundamental strategic options for growth. In innovation, the main debate is between the Classical advocates of market-oriented product development and the Processualists who doubt that truly significant advances can be legislated for. Systemic theorists find that marketeers do not dominate research and development in other successful economies, and wonder whether the nostrums of Anglo-Saxon marketing contain a touch of professional self-promotion. The Systemic perspective similarly suspects managerial self-interest as behind recent strategies of diversification and takeover. Evolutionists and Classicists, on the other hand, insist that the judgement of the market-place vindicates the basic efficiency of diversification. On internationalization, again Evolutionary theorists argue for the efficiency gains behind the surge in foreign direct investment in recent decades. Classical 'game theorists' think otherwise, seeing international moves and countermoves as an elaborate game designed to protect oligopolistic power. Systemic writers warn that the different social systems from which international competitors spring make a fundamental difference to competitive strategy across the globe.

Lastly, Chapter 6 considers how strategic options actually get carried out. Here Evolutionary and Classical theorists argue for the logic of organizational structure following business strategy. Processualists doubt that organizations in practice are really so plastic, and point to the reciprocal effect of organizational structures on strategic development. Systemic authors remind us that organizational structures do not necessarily follow the universalist logics of Evolutionary and Classical theory around the world. Processualists and Evolutionists clash again over the issue of strategic change. Here, the Processual advocates of cautious incrementalism and patient learning come face to face with the Evolutionists' ruthless reliance on market forces.

The final chapter reviews these different debates, summarizing the general implications of each approach both for the practice of strategic management and for government policy. This is the moment for you to choose which approach best fits your own experience, and then to build your own coherent strategic philosophy around it. The choice is quite stark: the four generic approaches to strategy differ fundamentally about what people are like and how they get on in the world which surrounds them. People are seen variously as objective calculating machines, muddled makers-do, or the particular products of their time and place, rational only according to the criteria of their peculiar culture or interests. The world in which they operate is portrayed by some as a simple series of markets to be conquered, by others as a jungle of fierce and unpredictable competition, or by still others as a complex interweaving of the social, the political and the economic. How you resolve these opposing views about people and the world in which they operate will deeply influence your own personal approach to strategy.

2 Theories of strategy

Practical men, who believe themselves to be quite exempt from any intellectual influences, are usually the slaves of some defunct economist. Madmen in authority, who hear voices in the air, are distilling their frenzy from some academic scribbler of a few years back.

(Keynes 1936: 383)

Introduction

The first chapter briefly introduced the four generic approaches to strategy, ranging them along the axes of Figure 1.1. Each approach has very different conceptions of what strategy is about and how actually to do it. This chapter explores the four in more detail, drawing out their basic assumptions, their intellectual pedigrees and their general implications for managerial practice. The chapter is theoretical – later chapters will address implications for specific strategic issues more directly.

Theories are important. They contain our basic assumptions about key relationships in business life. Theories tell us what to look out for, what our first steps should be, and what to expect as a result of our actions. Saving us from going back to first principles at each stage, they are actually short-cuts to action. Often these theories are not very explicit or very formal. Whether building from experience or from books, we all tend to have our own private assumptions about how things work, how to get things done. Providing the basic grounding for our behaviour, Argyris (1977) calls these assumptions 'theories of action'.

The danger of these theories is forgetting we have them. As Keynes (1936) implies, those who boast of their commonsense approach to management are very probably just following the ill-formed, half-forgotten, pseudo-scientific nostrums peddled to them in their early careers. Drawing upon his work with American senior managers, Argyris (1977) warns that nothing is more dangerous than to leave underlying assumptions hidden. Until we surface our implicit 'theories of action', we cannot test their accuracy and amend them to the conditions of the day. Those who do not actively confront their underlying assumptions are condemned to be 'prisoners of their own theories' (Argyris 1977: 119).

The point of this chapter, then, is to make explicit the assumptions that underlie the four basic theories of strategy. Each theory holds very different views about our human capacity to think rationally and act effectively. They diverge widely in their implications for strategic management. By directly confronting these differences, you should be better able to test your own 'theories of action' and to decide finally which basic theory most closely matches your own experience and needs.

Figure 2.1 **Summary implications of the four perspectives on strategy**

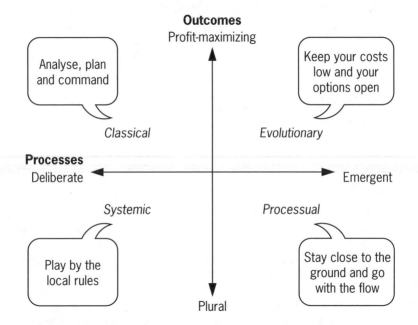

Before plunging into the detail, it is worth summarizing the general implications of each approach. For the Classical school, planning can adapt to and anticipate market change. Strategies are best made through rational analysis at one remove from the hurly-burly of the business battlefield itself. For the Evolutionists, markets are too tough and too unpredictable for heavy investments in strategic plans. They caution strategists to keep their costs low and their options open. The Processualists too challenge the detached approach of the Classicists: effective strategies emerge directly from intimate involvement in the everyday operations and basic strengths of the organization. Finally, Systemic approaches argue that strategies must be 'sociologically efficient', appropriate to particular social contexts. From a Systemic perspective, there is no one best way of strategy: just play by the local rules.

The Classical approach to strategy

For Classicists, profitability is the supreme goal of business, and rational planning the means to achieve it. Dominant in the mainstream textbooks, the Classical approach draws wide disciplinary and metaphorical support. Its notions of strategy formulation are informed by the economics of eighteenth-century Scotland, while its assumptions about strategic implementation appeal back to the militaristic ideals of Ancient Greece.

For all this, the Classical approach to business strategy is still novel. The beginnings of a coherent discipline only emerged in the 1960s, with the writings of business historian Alfred Chandler (1962), theorist Igor Ansoff (1965) and the businessman Alfred Sloan (1963). These three men early established the key features of the Classical approach: the attachment to rational analysis, the separation of conception from execution, and the commitment to profit maximization.

Alfred Sloan, former President of General Motors, defined the fundamental strategic problem as positioning the firm in those markets in which maximum profits could be earned. In his great biography *My Years with General Motors*, Sloan laid down the Classical profit-orientated goal of strategy:

> *the strategic aim of a business is to earn a return on capital, and if in any particular case the return in the long run is not satisfactory, the deficiency should be corrected or the activity abandoned.*
>
> (1963: 49)

Sloan's (1963) biography chronicles in detail the development of the measures and methods by which, with as much cold objectivity as he could summon, he pursued this strategic aim over four decades at General Motors. Among the innovations he helped to pioneer were return on investment criteria, the decentralized divisional form and the separation of 'policy' from operations (see 'Alfred Sloan and the "policy" concept').

Alfred Sloan and the 'policy' concept

General Motors was formed by William Durant during 1908 and 1909 by the merger of his own Buick company with Olds, Oakland and Cadillac to form the largest car manufacturer in the United States. By 1910, Durant had no less than twenty-five companies under his control, but his new empire ran quickly into financial difficulties and the bankers removed him from management. Nothing daunted, Durant launched a new company, Chevrolet, whose success helped bring him back to the top of General Motors in 1916. Again Durant launched a rush of acquisitions, including in 1918 the takeover of the Hyatt bearings company, run by Alfred Sloan.

Durant's entrepreneurial management style – which Sloan (1963: 52) characterized as 'seat of the pants' – drove General Motors into a second crisis during the 1920 recession. Pierre Du Pont, representing his large family shareholding, took over the presidency, and Sloan became his right-hand man. Three years later, Sloan became president himself: he was to remain at the top of the largest corporation in the world, latterly as chairman, until 1956.

Sloan (1963: xxvii) believed in the 'factual approach to business judgment'. During the 1920s, in parallel with similar reforms at Du Pont, General Motors pioneered the multidivisional form of organization and the concept of return on investment. With no existing precedents for organizing a diversified business as large as General Motors, Sloan's (1963: 56) approach was cerebral: 'short on experience, we were long on logic . . .'.

Sloan blamed General Motors' early crises on Durant's lack of an overall, long-term strategic view. His fundamental innovation, therefore, was his recognition of the need for strategy, which he called 'policy', and the importance of keeping it separate from the day-to-day business of operations. In an internal General Motors memorandum of 1934, Sloan (1963: 182) enunciated two influential principles: first, that 'the development or creation of constructive and advanced policies . . . is of vital influence in the progress and stability of the business', and second, that '[this] should be recognized through a specialization of policy creation, independent of policy execution'. In General Motors, 'policy' became the sole responsibility of the top Executive Committee and its advisory Policy Groups, from which divisional managers were rigorously excluded. This elevation of 'policy' was to become a fundamental hallmark of Classical thinking.

Sloan's example was highly influential. The prolific author and management consultant Peter Drucker worked for General Motors between 1943 and 1945, when the company employed half a million people. He subsequently publicized Sloan's management structures and style in two books, *The Concept of the Corporation* (1946; republished in 1973) and *Big Business* (1947). Igor Ansoff too was much impressed by Sloan, citing his statement on the strategic aim of business at the head of the first chapter of his *Corporate Strategy*, the first ever strategy textbook (a generation later, Grant (1991a: 16) reproduced the same statement in his first chapter). Sloan was also closely connected with the first academic researcher of strategy, historian Alfred D. Chandler. Chandler (1962) took General Motors as one of his four central case studies in his historical account of the evolution of strategy and structure in American business; his research was financed by the Sloan Research Fund; and he was himself – full name Alfred Du Pont Chandler – connected to the family which owned a quarter of Sloan's General Motors (the Du Pont company supplied the second of his four cases).

It may not be surprising, then, that Chandler shares Sloan's faith in the superiority of the top-down, planned and rational approach to strategy-making. Chandler's (1962) own influential definition of strategy has all the characteristics of Classical strategy thought: the emphasis on the long run, the explicit and deliberate conception of goals, and the logical cascading of actions and resources from original objectives. According to Chandler (1962: 13), strategy is

the determination of the basic, long-term goals and objectives of an enter-
prise, and the adoption of courses of action and the allocation of resources
necessary for those goals.

(1962: 13)

The central problem of the companies Chandler studied was how to build the organizational structures that would allow top management to focus on their strategic responsibilities. The basic reason for the success of the multidivisional structure that all four of his companies adopted in the first half of this century 'was simply that it clearly removed the executives responsible for the destiny of the entire enterprise from the more routine operational activities and so gave them the time, information, and even psychological commitment for long-term planning and appraisal' (Chandler 1962: 309). Thus was strategy formulation and control confirmed as the prime task of the top manager, strategy implementation as the responsibility of the operational managers in the divisions.

Sloan, Chandler and Ansoff did not, of course, dream up the concept of strategy from scratch. Ansoff (1965: 105) links his notion of strategy directly to both military practice and academic economics. Since then, economistic ideas about rational optimization, and militaristic expectations of hierarchical command, have continued to resonate in Classical thinking about strategy formulation and implementation.

Indeed, Bracker (1980) traces the concept of strategy to the Greek word *strategos*, 'a general', which in turn comes from roots meaning 'army' and 'lead'. Apparently, the link between military and business practice came early, when Socrates consoled Nichomachides, a Greek soldier who had lost an election to the position of general to a mere businessman. According to Bracker (1980: 219), Socrates explained to Nichomachides that the duties of a general and a businessman were equivalent: both involve planning the use of one's resources in order to meet objectives.

It is not clear that Nichomachides was consoled by this view, but anyway this military concept of business strategy was lost with the fall of the Greek city-states. There is no direct line of descent to modern business: Hoskin (1990) emphasizes the disjuncture between Greek military theory, tactical and partial in fact, and modern business strategy, long term and comprehensive in aspiration. None the less, as Hoskin (1990) finds, many of the earliest managerial systematizers of American business shared military origins, in particular training at the officer cadet school of West Point in the first half of the nineteenth century. Even today, when business strategy can claim a substantial and independent body of experience, military imagery continues to influence contemporary strategy analysis, as can be seen in the popularity of such books as James's (1985) *Business Wargames*. Certainly, the military metaphor reinforces several typical features of Classical approaches to strategy.

At the centre of the military tradition of strategy is the heroic yet slightly isolated figure of the general himself. Presiding at the top of a rigid hierarchy, it is the general who ultimately makes the decisions. From Alexander to Rommel, individual genius is critical to victory. Plans are conceived in the general's tent, overlooking the battlefield but sufficiently detached for safety. These preconceived plans are executed according to commands transmitted through obedient hierarchies to the officers and their men at the front: it is not for them to reason why, but simply to execute their orders. The men are sent to do battle, and the objective is simple: victory. Conflict, not co-operation, is the norm. The epitome of this coolly detached, sequential approach to strategy was General Colin Powell, chairman of the Joint Chiefs of Staff during the Gulf crisis. Asked how he planned to retake Iraqi-occupied Kuwait, he said: 'Our strategy for dealing with this [Iraqi] army is simple: first we are going to cut it off, then we're going to kill it' (*Sunday Times* 13 January 1991).

For the Classical theorists, this military model is complemented by an intellectual inheritance from economics. Indeed, the first academic application of the notion of strategy to business was made by two mathematical economists, von Neumann and Morgenstern (1944), in their *Theory of Games and Economic Behavior*. Since then, as Rumelt *et al.* 's (1991) recent view makes clear, economics has supplied the strategy field with many basic techniques and concepts – most notably Michael Porter's (1980) industry structure analysis and Oliver Williamson's (1985) concept of transaction costs in business organization.[1] However, the most pervasive contribution of economics to strategy is the philosophical core of assumptions summed up in the ideal type of 'rational economic man' (Hollis and Nell 1975).

The ideal of rational economic man projects strategy as the product of a single entrepreneurial individual, acting with perfect rationality to maximize 'his' economic advantage. Von Neumann and Morgenstern (1944) placed this singular figure right at the heart of their conception of strategy as an elaborate 'game' of move and counter-move, bluff and counter-bluff, between competing yet interdependent businesses.[2] Rational economic man was a necessary device. Only this reduction of the firm to a unique decision-maker would allow them to ignore internal organizational complexities; only this endowment of super-rationality would permit the sequence of mathematical calculations necessary to follow through the logics of the game.

Smuggled into Classical strategy thinking with the baggage of economics, the individualistic ideal of rational economic man goes back at least to the hard-headed economics of eighteenth-century Scotland. Hollander's (1988: 312) account of classical economics reveals how the fundamental principles of orthodox strategy thought were already present in the writings of Adam Smith. The profit-maximizing assumption is merely the economic expression of Smith's sad belief that self-interest was 'inherent in the very nature of our being'. Consequently, Smith asserted in his *Wealth of Nations* that 'each individual is continually exerting himself to find out the most advantageous employment of whatever capital he can command' – or, translated into the terms of modern accounting, each individual firm is continually exerting itself to maximize return on investment. According to Smith, our pursuit of this self-interest is governed by what he called 'prudence'. This notion of 'prudence' embodies the dual principles of 'reason' (the ability to foresee consequences and to discern advantage) and 'self-command' (the readiness to abstain from short-term opportunism in order to benefit more substantially in the long run) (Hollander 1988: 315–16). It is exactly these principles of eighteenth-century 'prudence' that are at the heart of modern long-term strategic planning.

Too Rational? Not prudent? Long Term Capital Management

The world of high finance has been taken over by 'rocket scientists' trading on quantitative models and the theory of rational expectations. In August 1998, one of the world's most sophisticated quantitative hedge funds, Long Term Capital Management (LTCM), lost over $2bn. when the world failed to conform to its sophisticated models.

LTCM's models could hardly have had a better source. The fund was advised by two Nobel laureates, the economists Robert Merton and Myron Scholes, inventors of option-pricing theory. The models exploited arbitrage opportunities in temporary disparities in the prices of related assets. So tiny were these disparities that it took big plays to make big bucks. So confident was LTCM in its models that it took on debts one hundred times its assets. Then it was hit by the unpredictable: simultaneous financial default by Russia and economic crisis in Asia. The normal relationships on which the models relied broke down and the fund went bankrupt.

Business Week observed that LTCM lacked 'street smarts'. They quoted one traditional Wall Street trader: 'I've seen too many of these quant geniuses that don't have a clue about how markets behave. When they get a shock like this, they're dumbfounded. They just don't have the intuition of what to do'.

Source: *Business Week*, 21 September, 1998.

The more pragmatic and self-conscious Classical thinkers hesitate over some of the economists' abstractions and the militarists' metaphors (see Grant 1991a: ch. 1). Yet echoes of both continue to linger in the orthodox textbooks. Henry Mintzberg's (1990) recent critique of strategic management orthodoxy exposes this subtext with painful clarity.[3]

By careful analysis of key texts, especially those associated with Harvard Business School, Mintzberg (1990) identifies what he terms the 'basic premises' of Classical thought. The first premise, that strategy formation should be a controlled conscious process of thought, derives directly from the notion of rational economic man. The premise that responsibility for control and consciousness must rest with the chief executive officer – 'THE strategist', as Mintzberg (1990: 176) puts it – reflects both the individualism of economics and the military notion of the solitary general at the tip of the pyramid of command. Military notions of command also inform the premise that strategies emerge from the decision-making process fully formulated, explicit and articulated: strategies are in a sense orders for others to carry out. Thence too comes Mintzberg's (1990) last premise, that implementation is a distinct phase in the strategy process, only coming after the earlier phase of explicit and conscious formulation. It is this which underlies the image of the strategist as general in his tent, despatching orders to the front. The actual carrying-out of orders is relatively unproblematic, assured by military discipline and obedience.

In sum, the Classical approach to strategy places great confidence in the readiness and capacity of managers to adopt profit-maximizing strategies through rational long-term planning.[4] Accordingly, the Classic texts from Ansoff (1965) to Grant (1991a) furnish us with an abundant technology of matrices, formulae and flowcharts. The 'seat-of-the-pants' managerial style of William Durant at General Motors is banished to the past. Flattered by the image of Olympian detachment, lured by the promise of technique-driven success, managers are seduced into the Classical fold.

Evolutionary perspectives on strategy

Evolutionary approaches to strategy are less confident about top management's ability to plan and act rationally. Rather than relying on managers, they expect markets to secure profit maximization. Stressing competitive processes of natural selection, Evolutionary theorists do not necessarily prescribe rational planning methods; rather, they argue that whatever methods managers adopt, it will only be the best performers that survive. Managers need not be rational optimizers because 'evolution is nature's cost-benefit analysis' (Einhorn and Hogarth 1988: 114).

Evolutionary theorists often make an explicit parallel between economic competition and the natural law of the jungle. Bruce Henderson, founder of the Boston Consulting Group, complains:

> *Classical economic theories of competition are so simplistic and sterile that they have been less contributions to understanding than obstacles. These theories postulate rational, self-interested behavior by individuals who interact through market exchanges in a fixed and static legal system of property and contracts.*

(1989: 143)

According to Henderson, these postulates are too abstract and unrealistic. Competition is not a matter of detached calculation but a constant struggle for survival in an over-populated, dense and steamy jungle. He concludes (1989: 143): 'Human beings may be at the top of the ecological chain, but we are still members of the ecological community. That is why Darwin is probably a better guide to business competition than economists are.'

In fact, many economists had reached a similar conclusion long before Bruce Henderson. R. C. Hall and Hitch's (1939) simple field enquiries had discovered that business practice was far from that prescribed by the ideal of rational economic man: not only did managers fail to set output at the theoretically profit-maximizing level where marginal costs exactly equal marginal revenues, but they had no idea what their marginal cost and revenue curves were anyway. Economists adjusted to this business stupidity by letting the markets do the thinking.

Thus Alchian (1950) appealed directly to the biological principle of natural selection to propose an evolutionary theory of the firm that downgraded managerial strategy and emphasized environmental fit. The most appropriate strategies within a given market emerge as competitive processes allow the relatively better performers to survive and flourish, while the weaker performers are irresistably squeezed out of the ecological niche. The evolution of industries typically follows the pattern of the French and United Kingdom automobile industries illustrated in Figure

Figure 2.2 **Populations of automobile manufacturers in France and the United Kingdom, 1885–1965**

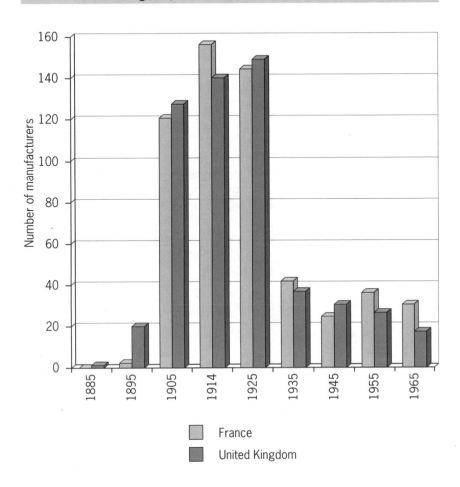

France

United Kingdom

Source: Adapted from Hannan 1997.

2.2. As a new niche opens up, it is initially flooded by new entrants, but then overpopulation drives a process of fierce competition that allows only the most 'fit' to survive (Hannan 1997). As Milton Friedman (1953) famously argued, it hardly matters if managers do not rationally profit-maximize so long as competitive markets ensure that only those who do somehow achieve the profit-maximizing position will survive over the long run. Markets, not managers, choose the prevailing strategies within a particular environment.

The Evolutionary economists initially emphasized competition in product markets as the means of winnowing out inefficient competitors.[5] Unfortunately, as critics such as Penrose (1952) were quick to remark, many large contemporary firms dominate the markets that are supposed to discipline them, with sufficient oligopolistic power to be well buffered against competitive pressures. For these companies, strategy is about selecting markets, rather than being selected by markets. More recent elaborations of Evolutionary theory (e.g. Pelikan 1989) have therefore emphasized other markets, especially managerial labour markets, the market for capital and the market for corporate control, as selecting the best performers for survival. In this broader view, incompetent managers are eliminated as they fail to get promoted or hired, as they find themselves unable to get bank loans, or as falling share prices provoke either shareholder revolt or hostile takeover. Thus, by one market or another, the pressure for profit maximization is maintained.

Digital Darwinism

At the peak of the Internet boom at the end of the 1990s, Tim Koogle, Chief Executive of Yahoo!, warned: 'This is natural Darwinism. There are lots of companies on the Web, but there aren't many businesses'.

Former *Business Week* editor and Internet guru Evan Schwartz notes that the amount invested in internet IPOs (Initial Public Offerings) in the United States surged from $2bn to $20bn from 1998 to 1999. He goes on to quote Charles Darwin in *The Origin of the Species*: 'We forget that though food may now be superabundant, it is not so at all seasons of each recurring year'.

Darwin also had some advice

Many more individuals of each species are born than can possibly survive. Consequently, there is a frequently recurring struggle for existence, and it follows that any being, if it varies however slightly in any manner profitable to itself under the complex conditions of life, will have a better chance of surviving and thus be naturally selected.

The stern Victorian's message is simple: differentiate or die.

Sources: Schwarz 1999; *Digital Darwinism Quarterly*, March Madness 2000 edition.

Evolutionary theory has some intriguing implications for managerial strategy. Henderson (1989) draws directly from the biological 'principle of competitive exclusion' established by the Russian biologist Gause in 1934. Gause had found that when he put two small organisms of the same genus but different species in a jar with a limited supply of food, they would survive; however, if the two organisms were from the same species, with exactly the same amount of food, they would die. Coexistence is impossible if organisms make their living in an identical way. Henderson's (1989) conclusion is that business survival in a competitive environment depends on strategies of differentiation.

The challenge for strategy is that many Evolutionary theorists doubt the capacity of organizations to achieve differentiation and adaptation in a deliberate and sustainable way. As the dinosaurs found, complex biological organisms usually adapt more slowly than their environments. Human organizations are often the same. Drawing on Processual insights into the difficulties of managing change, Evolutionary theorists emphasize the limited capacity of organizations to anticipate and respond purposively to shifts in the environment. Aldrich (1979) argues that environmental fit is more likely to be the result of chance and good fortune, even error, than the outcome of deliberate strategic choice. Alchian (1950) too warns against overestimating the power of strategy. For him, firms are tossed about by unpredictable and uncontrollable market forces. Like plants which flourish because the wind blew their seeds onto the sunny side of a wall, business success is generally the result of happenstance – just being at the right place at the right time.

> *Among all competitors, those whose particular conditions happened to be* *most appropriate for testing and adoption will be 'selected' as survivors ...* *The survivors may appear to be those having* adapted *themselves to the* *environment, whereas the truth may well be that the environment has* adopted *them.*
>
> (Alchian 1950: 213–14; emphasis in the original)

Indeed, investing in long-term strategies can be counter-productive. Organizations maximize their chances of survival in the short term by achieving perfect fit against their current environment. In a competitive environment, flexibility is evolutionarily inefficient. Strategy is too expensive; the investor in long-term strategies of innovation, diversification and change can always be undercut by the short-term, inflexible low-cost producer. Competitive markets thus introduce a bias to strategic conservatism. According to Hannan and Freeman (1988: 25) 'Organizational selection processes favour organizations with relatively inert structures, organizations that cannot change strategy and structure as their environments change.'

Evolutionists not only insist that markets are typically too competitive for expensive strategizing and too unpredictable to outguess. They also hold that markets are too efficient to permit the creation of any sustainable advantage. In a competitive environment, elaborate strategies can only deliver a temporary advantage: competitors will be quick to imitate and erode any early benefits. Classical techniques in particular are unlikely to deliver permanent superiority. The market for such knowledge is too perfect. As McCloskey observes:

> *formal methods will not earn abnormally high profits for long. The for-* *mality makes them easy to copy. Going to business school is not a way to* *acquire immense wealth, because it is too easy to get in.*
>
> (1990: 128)

The market ensures that everybody else has access to Michael Porter's (1985) writings on competitive advantage too.

For Evolutionists, then, strategy can be a dangerous delusion. Except for the minority of firms with significant market power, the prosaic conclusion of Oliver Williamson (1991: 87) is simply that 'economy is the best strategy'. The only real comparative advantage is relative efficiency. Managers must concentrate on their costs, especially the 'transaction costs' of organizing and co-ordinating. Williamson writes:

> *a strategizing effort will rarely prevail if a program is burdened by significant cost excesses in production, distribution or organization. All the clever ploys and positioning, aye, all the king's horses and all the king's men, will rarely save a project that is seriously flawed in first-order economizing respects.*
>
> (1991: 75)

Williamson's advice, then, is not to get distracted from the basics.

If deliberate strategizing is ineffective, then what matters is an abundance of diverse new initiatives from which the environment can select the best. Hannan and Freeman's (1988) 'population ecology' perspective suggests that overall efficiency can best be secured by ensuring a steady stream of new entrants into any organizational population, from which the relatively ill-adapted are ruthlessly selected out. Rates of new firm formation and failure, therefore, are equal and complementary indicators of economic health and dynamism. Thus the helter-skelter rise in the number of business failures in the United States – multiplying eightfold between 1980 and 1997 (Figure 2.3) – merely reflects the more effective natural selection processes brought about by competitive markets. The rise in new business start-ups over the same period has kept the American economy's 'gene pool' refreshed and replenished. It is little use trying to prop up and reform existing underperformers. Firms that are poorly adapted to current conditions should simply make way to let new businesses try their chances at achieving environmental fit. Market convert Tom Peters (1992: 618) actually applauds high business failure rates.

Figure 2.3 Darwinian America: business starts and failures in the United States

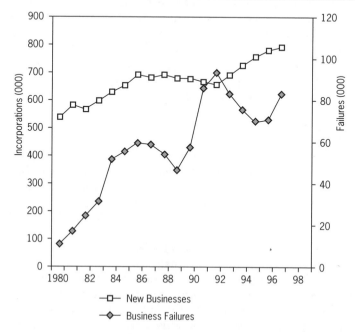

New Businesses

Business Failures

Source: Economic Report to the President; www.dnb.com:
note expanded coverage 1984 onwards.

The Evolutionary perspective clearly has rather gloomy implications for strategy. Certainly, differentiation is a sound principle within a competitive environment, but it is doubtful whether this can be achieved deliberately or permanently. The construction of grand long-term strategies may be so much vain distraction; managers would do much better to get down to the modest business of making sure that what they do now is done as efficiently as possible. If managers must attempt to anticipate change, then they would be wise not to try to outguess the market by investing heavily in a single major plan. The most effective approach may be to experiment with as many different small initiatives as possible, to wait and see which flourish and which fail, and then to build on the successes whilst ruthlessly eliminating the failures. It was this Darwinian approach that guided Sony in its strategy during the 1980s, when it launched more than 160 different Walkman versions in the American market, never retaining more than about twenty versions on the market at the same time (Sanchez and Sudharshan 1992). The Evolutionary advice, then, is that, in searching for the best strategy, it is best to let the environment do the selecting, not the managers.

Processual approaches to strategy

Processual approaches to strategy generally share the Evolutionary scepticism about rational strategy-making, but are less confident about markets ensuring profit-maximizing outcomes. For Processualists, both organizations and markets are often sticky, messy phenomena, from which strategies emerge with much confusion and in small steps. Indeed, they argue that it is to the very imperfections of organizational and market processes that managers owe their strategies and competitive advantages. The best Processual advice is not to strive after the unattainable ideal of rational fluid action, but to accept and work with the world as it is.

The foundations for the Processual approach were laid by the innovative work of the American Carnegie School – most prominently, Richard Cyert, James March and Nobel Prize-winner Herbert Simon. Together, they advanced a model of strategy-making that is still being restated with radical claims to novelty more than four decades later. Rejecting the specious unit of rational economic man on the one hand and the perfections of competitive markets on the other, they were led to take the internal complexity of organizations seriously. Here they uncovered two of the themes that have now become fundamentals of Processual thought: the cognitive limits on rational action, since extended by Henry Mintzberg (1987, 1994) in particular; and the micro-politics of organizations, developed by Andrew Pettigrew (1973, 1985).

Aiming for a more psychologically realistic theory of human behaviour, the Carnegie School emphasized the limits of human cognition. Rational economic man is a fiction: in practice, people are only 'boundedly rational' (Cyert and March 1963). By this they mean that we are unable to consider more than a handful of factors at a time; we are reluctant to embark on unlimited searches for relevant information; we are biased in our interpretation of data; and finally we are prone to accept the first satisfactory option that presents itself, rather than insisting on the best (March and Simon 1958; Cyert and March 1963). Even momentary consideration of our everyday behaviour will probably confirm the basic plausibility of these assumptions. The result is that the environmental scanning, data analyses and calculated comparisons of strategic options advocated by Classical theorists of strategy tend always to be flawed and incomplete. This is just human nature.

The micro-political view of organizations was established by the Carnegie School's recognition of the individual interests represented in any enterprise. Firms are not united in optimizing a single utility, such as profit. Rather, they are coalitions of individuals each of whom brings their own personal objectives and cognitive biases to the organization. Organizational members bargain between each other to arrive at a set of joint goals more or less acceptable to them all. The bargaining process involves both many compromises and what Cyert and March (1963: 31) describe as 'policy sidepayments' in return for agreement. For example, the Production Director may accept a reduced investment programme in order to secure at least some new machines this year, while supporting the Technical Director's bid for a new research and development initiative in electronics just to keep her on-side. Strategy is thus the product of political compromise, not profit-maximizing calculation.

The combination of political bargaining and bounded rationality strongly favours strategic conservatism. The need for change will only be imperfectly recognized, and anyway change is suspected because it is likely to set off a period of internal civil war until a new 'dominant coalition' is established (Cyert and March 1963). Strategic behaviour therefore tends to become entrenched in the 'routines' and 'standard operating procedures' imposed by political exigency and cognitive limits. Rather than perfectly rational strategies, organizations opt simply for 'adaptive rationality', the gradual adjusting of routines as awkward messages from a dynamic environment eventually force themselves on managers' attention.

Cyert and March (1956) argued that firms can get away with these slow adjustments because, contrary to the views of the more stringent Evolutionists, markets are in fact typically quite tolerant of underperformance. Firms often enjoy sufficient market power to be able to earn reasonable profits without maximum effort. Shareholders are unable to detect this underperformance because, like everybody else, they are not rational or informed enough to know. Thus firms can build sufficient 'organizational slack' to buffer themselves against the need for strategic change, delivering just enough profits to keep everybody reasonably happy. In this sense, firms 'satisfice' rather than profit-maximize (Cyert and March 1963: 41).

This modest view of organizations and the people who run them has significant implications for strategy. The Processual perspective radically downgrades the importance of rational analysis; it limits the search for strategic flexibility; and it reduces expectations of success. In practice, strategy-makers do not strive ceaselessly for the optimal solution, but satisfy themselves with following the established routines and heuristics of the organization. Indeed, as Nelson and Winter (1982: 133) observe, 'according to the concept of strategy that has been developed by a number of investigators associated with the Harvard Business School, the fundamental heuristic imperative for top management is: Develop a strategy'.

But strategy statements themselves can become routinized heuristics, working to constrain the field of opportunity and guiding decisions into established paths. Say Nelson and Winter, in strong Processual mood:

> *it is quite inappropriate to conceive of firm behavior in terms of deliberate choice from a broad menu of alternatives that some external observer considers to be 'available' opportunities for the organization. The menu is not broad, but narrow and idiosyncratic; it is built into the firm's routines, and most of the 'choosing' is also accomplished automatically by these routines.*

(1982: 134)

Strategies are not chosen; they are programmed.

Strategies, then, are a way in which managers try to simplify and order a world which is too complex and chaotic for them to comprehend. The regular procedures and precise quantifications of strategic planning are comforting rituals, managerial security blankets in a hostile world. Thus Weick (1990) tells the story of a Hungarian detachment that got lost in the Alps during military manoeuvres. As it snowed for two days, the soldiers despaired and laid themselves down to die in the frozen wilderness. Then suddenly one of the soldiers found a map in his pocket, the detachment took heart, and they marched confidently out of the mountains. Safe back at camp, they discovered the map was of the Pyrenees. For Weick (1990), strategic plans are often like this map: it does not matter much if they are wrong, so long as they give managers the confidence and sense of purpose to act. If the firm sits waiting for the right map, it will freeze; if it gets up and moves, it will somehow or other find direction, acquire experience and make its own opportunities.

In this way, the Classic sequence of formulation first, implementation second, gets reversed: strategy is discovered in action (March 1976). Alfred Sloan's (1963) distinction between 'policy creation' and 'policy execution' begins to blur. Doubting top managers' capacity to prescribe effective strategies in the splendid isolation of their executive suites, Mintzberg (1987) proposes the metaphor of strategy as 'craft'.[6] The craftswoman is intimately involved with her materials: she shapes her clay by personal touch, imperfections inspire her to artistic improvisation, hands and mind work together in a process of constant adaptation. So should it be with strategy. In a world too complex and full of surprises to predict, the strategist needs to retain the closeness, the awareness and the adaptability of the craftsperson, rather than indulging in the hubris of grand long-range planning. For Mintzberg, crafting strategy is a continuous and adaptive process, with formation and implementation inextricably entangled.

This view of strategy is an unglamorous one: hands get dirty, steps are small and there are few bold lunges into the unknown long term. But this slow progress is not to be despised. As Lindblom (1959) claimed, there is 'a science of muddling through', involving cautious comparison of successive options and careful maintenance of consensus. The gradual adaptive approach to strategy has its own rationality, which Quinn (1980: 89) terms 'logical incrementalism'. The superior rationality of logical incrementalism lies in its acceptance of our own bounded rationality: 'Smart strategists appreciate that they cannot always be smart enough to think through everything in advance' (Mintzberg 1987: 69). Honest about his or her limits, the logical incrementalist is committed to a process of experimentation and learning.

Surfing the edge of chaos

The notion of 'emergence' in strategy finds increasing support in 'chaos theory', the new science of complex adaptive systems. This new science is concerned with how order tends naturally to spring from chaos. It doesn't take precise planning from the top, only a few simple rules guiding action from the bottom.

Brown and Eisenhardt (1999) give the example of 'boids' – a computer simulation of autonomous, bird-like agents. Something remarkable happens when these mindlessly moving agents are given just three simple rules: try to maintain a minimum distance from other objects, including other boids; try to match the velocity of nearby boids; and try to move to the centre of the mass of nearby boids. Regardless of their starting positions on the screen, and of the number and positioning of obstacles, the boids always end up doing the same thing: forming a flock. There's no need for leaders; order emerges naturally from myriads of small adaptive adjustments.

The point about being on the 'edge of chaos' is to have enough structure to allow for patterns to emerge, but not so much as to cause inflexibility and cost. The American company 3M allows scientists to do whatever they like with 15 per cent of their time, but within a framework that insists on taking 30 per cent of sales from products less than four years old while imposing tough targets for profit and growth. Innovative ideas – such as the Post-it or Thinsulate – bubble up from below but fall into place within a coherent strategic frame. Surfing on the edge of chaos means riding the wave – never falling behind and never falling in.

Sources: Brown and Eisenhardt 1999; Pascale 1999.

The incrementalist approach is not necessarily a tactical one. It may be informed by an underlying logic, or 'strategic intent', that is both sufficiently clear to provide a sense of direction and sufficiently broad to allow flexibility and opportunism along the way as for instance Komatsu's ambition simply to 'encircle Caterpillar' (Hamel and Prahalad 1989). More radically, Mintzberg and Waters (1985) suggest, the underlying strategic logic may be perceived only after the event. Strategies are often 'emergent', their coherence accruing through action and perceived in retrospect. Thus Intel's famous switch from the Dynamic Random Access Memories (DRAMs) market to its new role as a dominant player in microprocessors was achieved during the 1980s through an accumulating series of incremental investment decisions that had consistently valued the prospects of the new business more highly than the old. Yet all the while the company's explicit strategy and self-definition was still to be a 'memory company', its original business. As late as 1985, one third of the research and development budget was still devoted to the 'strategically important' memory business, even when the company had been reduced to a negligible 2 to 3 per cent market share. As Chief Executive Officer Andy Grove observed: 'Don't ask managers "What is your strategy?" Look at what they do!' (Burgelman 1996: 423).

This incremental approach to strategy is reinforced by Processualists who emphasize the stickiness of external markets. For the 'resource-based' strategy theorists (e.g. Grant 1991b), market imperfections inhibit the opportunity-maximizing strategies proposed by Classicists. The resources with which firms compete are not all to be bought and sold in markets according to the shifting matrix of strategic opportunities and threats (Collis and Montgomery 1995). Resource-based theories of the firm stress how a firm's resources include tacit skills, patterns of co-operation, and intangible assets that take time and learning to evolve. These resources cannot be traded, changed or imitated with ease. The origin of a firm's competitive advantage, therefore, lies in what is unique and embedded in its resources – these constitute its core, distinctive competences (Grant 1991b).

In other words, the sources of sustainable superior performance lie internally, in the capacity to exploit and renew distinctive resources, rather than externally, in simply positioning the firm in the right markets. Strategy involves building on core competences, not chasing each and every opportunity. Hamel (1991: 83) accuses: 'the traditional "competitive strategy" paradigm (e.g. Porter 1980), with its focus on product-market positioning, focuses on only the last few hundred yards of what may be a skill-building marathon'. However attractive market opportunities might be, entry strategies will fail in the implementation if the firm lacks the requisite skills and resources internally or underestimates the difficulty of acquiring them externally. What matters in strategy, therefore, is the long-term construction and consolidation of distinctive internal competences. In this view, strategy becomes a patient inwardly aware process, rather than the fluid externally oriented pursuit of opportunity emphasized by Classical industry structure analyses.

The knowledge resource

In today's knowledge-based economy, superior knowledge is likely to be the most valuable resource of all. Knowledge is valuable precisely because it is hard to manage and hard to trade. Most useful knowledge is tacit, not easily captured in managerial databases or imitated by competitors. Knowledge resides inside the heads of lower ranking staff, not in the files of top management. Knowledge is dynamic in unpredictable ways – experience and events are always adding to it, regardless of formal efforts at research and development. Knowledge is hard to trade, because the acquirer cannot know its value until it is actually used. Knowledge is often highly immobile, because embedded in the routines, culture and teams of a particular organization. For all these reasons, the value of knowledge is unlikely to diffuse away through normal processes of market competition and exchange.

> Equally, all these knowledge characteristics impose constraints on the strategy process. Especially in knowledge-intensive firms, such as professional services or new technology enterprises, strategy is as likely to emerge bottom-up as top-down. After all, it is at the bottom where the knowledge lies and is continuously recreated. Top managers ignore this source of value in their strategy process at their peril.
>
> Sources: Conner and Prahalad 1996; Tsoukas 1996; Zack 1999.

Thus the Processualist focus on the imperfections of organizational and market processes yields at least four conceptions of strategy radically different from the Classical perspective: strategy may be a decision-making heuristic, a device to simplify reality into something managers can actually cope with; plans may just be managerial security blankets, providing reassurance as much as guidance; strategy may not precede action but may only emerge retrospectively, once action has taken place; strategy is not just about choosing markets and then policing performance, but about carefully cultivating internal competences. Many of the confident precepts of the Classicists are put in jeopardy: suddenly, it seems that goals are slippery and vague, long-term policy statements vain delusions, and the separation of formulation from implementation a self-serving top management myth.

For the pure Processualists of the Carnegie School, all this means that strategy is inescapably about satisficing, settling for less than the optimal. But more managerial Processualists turn the messy reality of organizations and markets to advantage. In practice, the technical sophistication of the Classicists amounts to naive idealism. It is above all by recognizing and accommodating real-world imperfections that managers can be most effective. Giving due attention to implementation, exploiting imperfect markets to build distinctive competences, cultivating flexibility for incremental adaptation – these are really the means to maximum performance.

Systemic perspectives on strategy

Against the sometimes nihilistic propositions of Evolutionary and Processual theorists, Systemic theorists do retain faith in the capacity of organizations to plan forward and to act effectively within their environments. Where they differ from the Classicists, however, is in their refusal to accept the forms and ends of Classical rationality as anything more than historically and culturally specific phenomena. Systemic theorists insist that the rationales underlying strategy are peculiar to particular sociological contexts.

A central tenet of Systemic theory is that decision-makers are not simply detached calculating individuals interacting in purely economic transactions, but people rooted deeply in densely interwoven social systems. Granovetter's (1985) notion of social 'embeddedness' captures the sense that economic activity cannot be placed in a separate rarified sphere of impersonal financial calculation. In reality, people's economic behaviour is embedded in a network of social relations that may involve their families, the state, their professional and educational backgrounds, even their religion and ethnicity (Swedberg *et al.* 1987; Whittington 1992). These networks influence both the means and ends of action, defining what is appropriate and reasonable behaviour for their members. Behaviour that may look irrational or inefficient to the Classical theorist may be perfectly rational and efficient according to the local criteria and *modus operandi* of the particular social context.

Systemic theorists propose, therefore, that firms differ according to the social and economic systems in which they are embedded. They are not all perfect profit-maximizers, as they choose to be in Classical theory and they are obliged to be in Evolutionary theory. But nor are they just the particularistic organizations of the Processual perspective, whose idiosyncrasies are the product of internal limits and compromises. In the Systemic view, the norms that guide strategy derive not so much from the cognitive bounds of the human psyche as from the cultural rules of the local society. The internal contests of organizations involve not just the micro-politics of individuals and departments but the social groups, interests and resources of the surrounding context. The variables of the Systemic perspective include class and professions, nations and states, families and gender.

Important, therefore, to Systemic theory are differences between countries' social systems and changes within countries' social systems. As Whitley (1999) has shown for southeast Asia, prevailing forms of business may vary widely according to the local interplay of state, familial and market structures. Thus, in South Korea, a traditionally strong state has promoted the creation of the vast chaebol conglomerates; in nearby Taiwan, by contrast, the combination of an exclusionary Kuomintang state with the peculiar culture of Chinese family business has created an entrepreneurial economy of small and medium-sized firms, loosely linked by familial networks. Whitley (1991: 24) concludes: 'different kinds of enterprise structures become feasible and successful in particular social contexts, especially where cultures are homogeneous and share strong boundaries with nation states'. For all the contemporary talk of globalization, the peculiarities of local histories and local societies still matter.

Indeed, most large companies are hardly global at all. The Gestrin *et al.* (2000) survey of more than 200 Fortune Global 500 large corporations finds that on average roughly 60 per cent of their turnover and their assets were still concentrated in their home markets (see Figure 2.4). Growth in international turnover and assets had been slow throughout the 1990s and the profit share from overseas had been disproportionately weak even before the Asian crisis of 1997–98. The world's largest international engineering conglomerates illustrate the point: only 41 per cent of General Electric's sales in 1999 were outside the United States, 35 per cent of assets and just one third of profits (www.ge.com); at Hitachi, just 30 per cent of 1999 sales were outside Japan, 17 per cent of assets, but, so depressed was the Japanese market, 69 per cent of profits (www.hitachi.co.jp). In Hu's (1992) sceptical phrase, companies like these are not so much global multinationals as domestic companies with international subsidiaries.

Figure 2.4 **Average international scope of Fortune Global 500 firms**

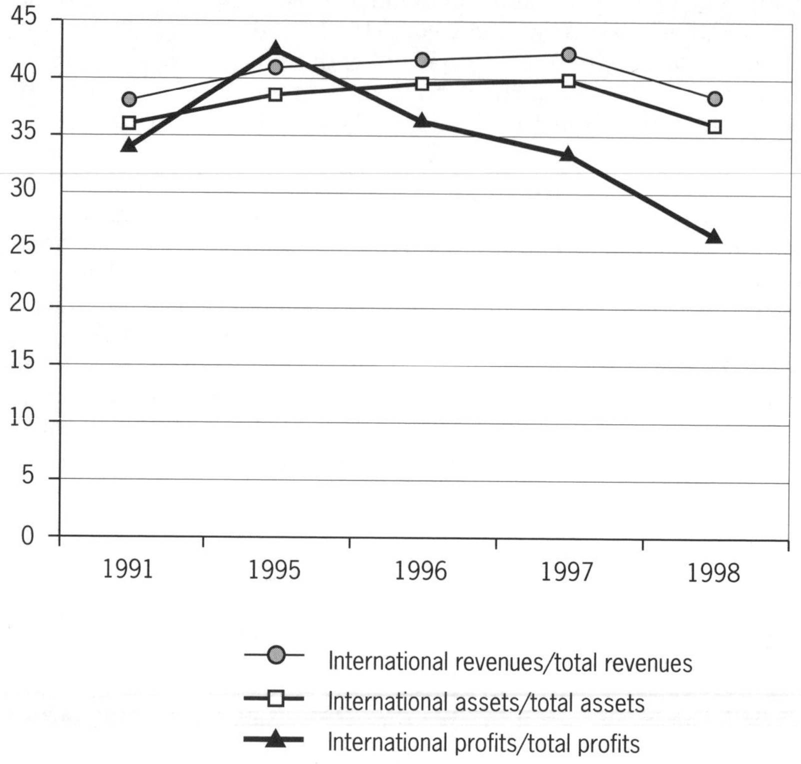

○— International revenues/total revenues
□— International assets/total assets
▲— International profits/total profits

Source: Gestrin *et al.* 2000.

Thus even the largest multinationals can retain strong local character. As Walker (1988: 395) observes, in its image and management style 'General Motors remains a thoroughly mid-western company'. Apple is very Californian. IKEA is Swedish. Companies – whether as competitors, customers, partners or suppliers – vary widely according to their local contexts. Rather than rising above their origins, even multinationals may be deeply influenced by the industrial cultures, class structures, politics and professional biases of their home nations.

Indeed, the very notion of 'strategy' may be culturally peculiar. Arising in the particular conditions of North America in the post-war period, the Classical conception of strategy does not always fit comfortably in other cultures. Pascale (1982) reports that the Japanese do not even have a phrase for 'corporate strategy'. 'Strategy' has strong connotations of free-will and self-control, but many cultures prefer to interpret events less as the product of deliberate human action, and more as the result of God, fate, luck or history (Boyacigiller and Adler 1991). For example, fundamentalist Muslims see life following a path pre-ordained by God, while the Chinese often explain events in terms of 'Joss', a combination of luck and fate. To these deterministic cultures, the idea of 'strategy' embodies a voluntarism that is entirely alien. Boyacigiller and Adler's (1991) analysis suggests that Classical notions of strategy are the product of a historically peculiar coincidence between the American 'can-do' culture and the steady growth and 'Pax Americana' of the 1950s and early 1960s. Strategy as a managerial practice developed in a context of cultural voluntarism and economic and political security that was uniquely favourable to long-term strategic planning.

The American origins of the strategy concept may also constrain our understanding of what strategy involves. Wilks (1990) finds that the Anglo-Saxon cultures of the United States and the United Kingdom are biased towards an individualistic free-enterprise model of strategy that denigrates explicit reliance upon the state. By contrast, the traditional nationalism of the French and German states, and the developmental role of the Japanese state, have given to the Anglo-Saxon world's major competitors industrial cultures in which the enlisting of state resources is seen as a natural and important part of strategic management (Wilks 1990). Thus national approaches to strategy can be heavily distorted by what is locally regarded as culturally legitimate.

From this perspective, the Classical and Evolutionary emphases on markets and profitability, to the exclusion of state resources and national interests, are simply the product of very particular historical and social circumstances. This is not to say that they are necessarily 'wrong'. The current sociological appreciation of the 'institutional environments' of organizations (Meyer and Rowan 1977; DiMaggio and Powell 1983) highlights the social pressures to conform to local forms of rationality. American business works within a culture which respects profit, values technical procedures and regards the free market as an article of faith. In this context, any individual business-leader who repudiates outright the forms of Classical strategy-making risks losing his or her credibility in the face of auditors, customers, financial markets and governmental regulators, all of whom can exert considerable influence on success. Whether or not formal planning in the Classical mode is economically effective, if that is how key elements of the institutional environment expect business to be done, then it is sociologically efficient to at least go through the motions. The rationality of the Classical approach to strategy may be a social construct, but nevertheless it is one that it can be dangerous to ignore.

Yet it remains important to be clear how particular conceptions of strategy reflect and reinforce the limitations of a particular society. Indeed, Shrivastava (1986) goes so far as to allege that the whole discipline of orthodox strategic management actually constitutes a self-servingly conservative political ideology. He points to how the Classic theorists' normative emphasis on top-down management and profit maximization as the ultimate unifying goal serves to reproduce the conditions of hierarchically organized capitalist society in general. The firm is typically represented as a 'co-operative system' (e.g. Barnard 1938), for whom the arrogation by top management of goal-setting and decision-making is merely a matter of administrative efficiency. Classical techniques of environmental analysis take the existing structures of society for granted and tend anyway to focus specifically on market factors, downplaying the relevance of social, cultural and political demands on the organization. Thus Michael Porter (1980: xix) blithely relegates his assumption of profit objectives to a footnote, and concentrates his industry analysis on five sets of economic forces amongst which government and labour are almost entirely lost.

Shrivastava (1986) concludes that orthodox strategic management is not a neutral, objective, scientific discipline, but an ideology that serves to normalize the existing structures of American society and universalize the goals of its dominant elite. Because it is designed to preserve the status quo, Classical strategic management traps strategists within a particularly narrow range of strategic options. To invoke state resources, or to challenge the top-down logic of strategic orthodoxy, is to play dangerously with the established social order.

The ideologies guiding strategy in different countries can be influenced strongly by different cultural traditions around the world. The American culture is hard-nosed and individualistic. In repeated surveys of international executives, Hampden-Turner and Trompenaars (1993) report that American attitudes stand out consistently from many of their competitors'. When asked whether the only goal of a company was profit, 40 per cent of American executives answered yes, against only 8 per cent from Japan and 11 per cent from Singapore. In a structured comparative analysis of American and South Korean managers' strategic decision-making criteria, project cash flow and return on investment were amongst the top three for the Americans. For the Koreans, it was sales growth and market share that were critical: cash-flow and cash-flow ranked tenth and eleventh out of thirteen possible criteria (Hitt *et al.* 1997). In its understanding of what matters in strategy, the United States is clearly something of an outlier. But it is American practice and American research that dominate strategy textbooks world-wide.

Figure 2.5 **Allianz's alliances (percentage shareholdings)**

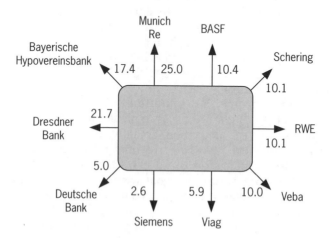

Source: *Financial Times*, 7 December 1999.

More than culture is involved in defining local approaches to strategy. Differences in strategy are so enduring, and patterns so hard to change, because they are also founded on real economic, social or political conditions. Recent analyses have explored the implications for strategy of different ownership structures in particular. The detached and relatively diffuse relationships between shareholders and their companies that are taken for granted in the Anglo-Saxon economies are unusual elsewhere round the world (Scott 1997). In the Germanic economies – Germany itself, Austria, Switzerland and to a lesser extent the Netherlands and Scandinavia – banks and other financial institutions play a central and interventionist role, with long-term relationships. For example, Deutsche Bank was a prime mover in bringing its two clients together to create the merged company Daimler Benz in 1926, and three quarters of a century later, it was still the largest shareholder in the new DaimlerChrysler company, holding 12 per cent in 1999 (Gall 1995; www.daimlerchrysler.com). Deutsche Bank also has a 9 per cent stake in the great German insurance company, Allianz, which reciprocates with a 5 per cent stake in the other direction. Although changes in German corporate law may prompt an unravelling, at the end of the twentieth century Allianz still occupied a central place in German capitalism, with substantial stakes in key utility companies, major chemicals and engineering companies, as well as the leading financial institutions (see Figure 2.5). Not very much happens in German business without the Allianz or its allies having a say.

Table 2.1 **European firms with shareholders above 5 per cent, by category** (domestically owned industrial top one hundred companies: does not sum to 100)

Per cent of firms	United Kingdom	France	Germany
None	52.2	7.6	11.1
Personal	4.5	42.4	46.0
Bank	5.9	13.6	20.6
Other financial institution	22.4	17.5	11.1
Other firm	10.4	30.3	14.3
State	1.5	24.4	9.5
Other	13.5	8.3	12.7

Source: Mayer and Whittington 1999.

The powerful role of the German financial institutions is part of systematic differences between countries in patterns of ownership. Table 2.1 indicates that, in 1993, more than half the largest industrial firms in the United Kingdom had no shareholder with more than 5 per cent of the shares, while in France and Germany the proportions were around a tenth. The table shows that the power of banks such as Deutsche Bank in Germany is replicated in France to some extent, where Crédit Lyonnais, Paribas and BNP play large roles. By contrast, in the United Kingdom banks held stakes above 5 per cent in only about one in twenty large corporations. Financial institutions such as the Prudential were important in the United Kingdom, but they rarely had stakes as large as typified by Allianz for Germany. France and Germany stand-out particularly for the continuing importance of personal ownership in their systems: around four out of every ten large companies have substantial personal (familial or entrepreneurial) stakes. The roll-call of large companies with substantial personal ownership includes such giants as LVMH, Michelin, Peugeot in France and Bertelsman, BMW and Siemens in Germany (Whittington and Mayer 2001). This kind of personal influence is not unusual. In Sweden, the Wallenberg family alone has major stakes in Ericsson, AstraZeneca, SAS, SKF and Volvo (*Business Week*, 30 August 1999). The Agnelli family still dominates Fiat, has influential stakes in the French food companies Danone and Saint Louis, as well as forming part of the controlling group in Italy's biggest bank, the Istituto Bancario San Paolo di Torino (*The Economist*, 25 April 1998). Further afield, the ten leading *chaebol* of South Korea – headed by such giants as Hyundai, Samsung and LG – still have average family ownership stakes of 35 per cent (*Far Eastern Economic Review*, 23 September 1999). In China, on the other hand, 34 per cent of the nation's output and no less than 110 million workers are accounted for by state-owned firms (Bruton *et al.* 2000).

Ownership can make a clear difference to strategy. At Jardine Matheson (see 'American capitalism versus 'Asian'?'), the controlling Keswick family attributed mediocre performance to the long-term view, while American investors blamed self-interest and incompetence. In a study of more than

American capitalism versus 'Asian'?

In June 2000, a nineteenth-century trading company, originating in the Chinese opium trade, defeated an American investment fund's challenge to the continuing control of its founding family.

The Keswick family has controlled Jardine Matheson, a large Hong Kong conglomerate, since 1874: Henry Keswick is the current chairman. The main mechanism of control has been cross-shareholdings between Jardine Matheson and a shell company, Jardine Strategic, created in 1986 in response to a hostile takeover bid from the Hong Kong tycoon Sir YK Pao. Jardine Matheson and Jardine Strategic share seven directors, constituting a majority on both boards. Through the cross-holdings, the Keswick family has voting control of Jardine Matheson while only owning 11 per cent of its shares.

Jardine Matheson shares, however, had been trading at a 20–30 per cent discount to net asset value, pointing to big gains from a potential break-up of the sleepy and unsuccessful group. Brandes Investment Partners from San Diego, with an 8 per cent stake, demanded that Jardine Strategic divest its majority stake in Jardine Matheson, leaving the company with no protective dominant shareholder. Henry Keswick argued against any such action aimed merely at producing 'a short-term increase in the share-price'. Doing business in Asia required the long-view that his family had always taken. The Keswicks mobilized the very voting power that Brandes had targeted in order to defeat the proposal.

Rodney Leach, a board member of both Jardine Matheson and Jardine Strategic, commented: 'Asia is different. You have to work within a society. It isn't always the American way'.

Sources: *Financial Times* 2 June 2000, 3 June 2000;
South China Morning Post 1 June 2000.

400 leading companies from across Western Europe, Thomsen and Pedersen (2000) found not only substantial family and state ownership, but important impacts on financial performance. Families and governments were associated with significant under-performance in simple financial terms, although families were also found to obtain faster rates of sales growth. Thomsen and Pedersen (2000: 703) conclude:

> *shareholder value does not appear to be a universal goal of corporate strategy . . . Strategists need to take into account the risk perceptions, time preferences, business relations, and social goals of large owners. Corporate strategies that do not match corporate governance are unlikely to be sustainable, because they lack backing from the ultimate decision-makers.*

Labour markets too can sustain systematically different approaches to strategy. Pascale (1984) has characterized the Japanese approach to strategy as one of 'adaptive persistence' and 'strategic accommodation', by contrast with the grand top-down analytical sweeps of Western theory. Thus, according to Pascale (1984), the success of Honda in the American small motorbike market was born not of a deliberate manipulation of the experience curve, as Classical theorists have claimed, but of dogged commitment to an overall goal and a readiness to learn. Despite failure with their large bikes, Honda persisted until, almost by chance, their small bikes took off and a new successful strategy suddenly emerged.

This learning approach is more than a cultural phenomenon. Aoki (1990) suggests that the Japanese preference for operational adaptation within broad indicative frameworks, rather than reliance on detailed prior planning, is an outcome of very specific labour market conditions. The ability to adjust strategies during implementation as information is fed back from operational units depends on a very able and committed blue-collar workforce. In the 1950s and 1960s, there were relatively few opportunities for further and higher education in Japan, so that between 25 and 45 per cent of males went straight into employment after junior high school. Although intelligent, these men were denied the chance to acquire portable qualifications that would give them labour market mobility and access to non-factory employment. Now that educational opportunities have improved, Japanese firms risk losing this supply of able and committed labour for their factories, thereby jeopardizing their capacity to adjust strategies flexibly as the result of operational learning. In short, the Systemic conditions underpinning the distinctive Japanese approach to strategy may be disappearing.

Thus the historical dynamics of particular societies make a difference to prevailing forms of strategy. The structures of Anglo-Saxon business in which Classical theory arose are still quite novel in the history of capitalism – and they are still developing. In particular, some Systemic theorists point to how changes in the social constitution of management itself may be leading to system-wide shifts in the rationalities informing strategic action.

Theorists of a new 'managerial capitalism' (Marris 1964; Berle and Means 1967) suggest a growing split between ownership and control within large Western companies. Since the 1920s, firms have increasingly been governed by professional managers rather than by their true owners. These theorists accuse managers of running their firms in their own interests, sacrificing profitability for the perquisites of growth. From this Systemic perspective, then, Alfred Sloan's Classic goal of maximizing return on investment has been superseded by managerial objectives such as security, empire-building, high rewards and high status. Abundant evidence for such managerial self-interest can be found in studies of top management compensation. The continuous upward spiral of chief executive rewards in America, despite chronically poor economic performance, certainly does not suggest that top management is as unselfishly dedicated to shareholders' interests as Classical theory likes to think (see 'Managerial rewards in the United States').

Managerial rewards in the United States

Top pay in America has rocketed during the last decade or so. Real profits have been much slower to grow. In 1999, the annual *Business Week* scoreboard puts the average total compensation of chief executives from 362 leading companies at $12.4 million, nearly twelve times the average fifteen years before. Over the same period, total corporate profits in the United States have increased just three times, to $835 billion (see Figure 2.6).

Figure 2.6 **Chief executive pay and profits in the United States**

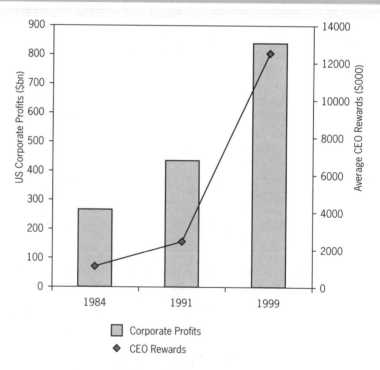

Corporate Profits
◆ CEO Rewards

Sources: *Business Week*, 6 May 1985, 4 May 1992, 7 April 2000;
US Department of Commerce.

These rewards do not always please shareholders. The highest paid chief executive in 1999 was Charles Wang, chairman and chief executive of Computer Associates, who received $655 million worth of stock in a single year. Scandalized financial markets responded by taking the stock value down by nearly half. A subsequent court challenge obliged Wang to hand about one third of the stock back to the company (*Business Week*, 17 April 2000).

These managerial rewards raise issues of internal equity too. The *Business Week* top executives are earning more than 300 times the average American manufacturing employee's total compensation, a relatively modest $40,000 per annum. It's hard for ordinary workers to believe that they and their bosses are all in it together.

Finally, these rewards can cause embarrassment internationally. When Daimler-Benz took over Chrysler in 1998, it was found that the top ten German managers had earned $11 million dollars between them the previous year. At Chrysler, Chairman Bob Eaton and Vice-Chairman Bob Lutz alone had shared a comfortable $26 million (*Wards Auto World*, June 1998). The ratio of average chief executive pay to average manufacturing employee pay is three times higher in the United States than in Germany or Japan (Towers Perrin World Remuneration Report 1999).

The rise of professional management has prompted Knights and Morgan (1990, 1991) to give a different twist to Shrivastava's (1986) argument: according to them, the discipline of 'strategy' reflects the ideological needs of the professional managerial class in particular, rather than those of capital as a whole. Knights and Morgan (1990) recall how the notion of military strategy, lost after the demise of the Ancient Greeks, was retrieved by the professional generals and military staff of early nineteenth-century Prussia. This Prussian officer class was historically unprecedented in that its claim to leadership was based not on the blue-blood of aristocracy but on scientific expertise in warfare. Theorists such as von Clausewitz constructed a discourse of strategy that was both technically effective and, at least as important, provided middle-class professionals with a legitimate basis for their new power.

Knights and Morgan (1990) observe that the discourse of strategy entered the business world too at a time of changes in class dominance. Until the 1950s, entrepreneurial capitalists had managed perfectly well for centuries without the concept of 'corporate strategy'. But during the post-war period, just as in the nineteenth-century Prussian army, control in American business was shifting – out of the traditional hands of owners and into the hands of middle-class professionals. While owners could rely on the established rights of ownership, these new professional managers had to construct claims to legitimacy of their own. Like the Prussian officer-class, they found justification for their power by inventing the discipline of business strategy. Knights and Morgan (1990: 477) conclude: 'In this sense, strategy is part of a discourse of power which reproduces certain sets of hierarchical sets of social relationships through legitimating them with reference to positivistic and scientifistic norms of rationality.'

Whether practically effective or not, the point about the formally rational apparatus of Classical strategy-making is that it cloaks managerial power in the culturally acceptable clothing of science and objectivity.

Systemic approaches, then, emphasize how strategic goals and processes reflect the social systems in which strategy is being made. Variations in market, class, state and cultural systems make a difference to corporate strategy. Not all firms within a particular social system need be the same, however. Societies are too complex and people too individualistic to expect bland uniformity. Neither Japanese enterprises nor professional managers will always behave in just the same way. The rich complexity of most societies offers a plurality of resources and norms of conduct, capable of enabling and legitimating a wide range of business behaviours. Individual strategists are able to build from the diverse and plural features of their particular social systems unique and creative strategies of their own.

For example, in her study of direct sales organizations in the United States, Biggart (1989) shows that firms such as Amway ('the American Way') or Mary Kay Cosmetics reject Classical bureaucratic rationality and instead draw on American notions of patriotism or sisterhood to inspire strategies of evangelical zeal. However economically peculiar these businesses may seem, they can coexist successfully with more orthodox competitors because their practices are legitimate within an institutional environment that values the American flag and traditional family roles as much as the formal rationality of Classical management. Likewise, the strategic orientations of Taiwanese computer manufacturers are influenced by the competing internal logics of Taiwanese society (Hung and Whittington 1997). Acer and Twinhead, for example, have both been very close to the Kuomintang political regime, with at one point Taiwan's President a substantial shareholder in Acer and the Kuomintang a shareholder in Twinhead. Accordingly, both companies have followed strategies of branding, innovation and internationalization favoured by the government, while resisting the temptations of importing cheap labour or locating production in China, policies opposed by the government. On the other hand, many large Taiwanese computer manufacturers – such as FIC, a member of the Formosa Group – are much less closely connected to the regime, or even opposed, and have therefore followed the traditional Taiwanese practices of manufacturing for better-known foreign companies and ruthlessly cutting costs, either through immigrant labour or disfavoured Chinese manufacturing facilities. In other words, strategists can play different games according to the plural rules of their societies. They may be embedded in society, but they are not all embossed with the same stamp (Whittington 1992).

For practising managers, then, the special advantage of the Systemic approach lies in its heightened sociological sensitivity. By alerting individual managers to the key elements of the social systems in which they work, the Systemic approach can widen the search for resources and deepen the appreciation of competitors. Every strategist should analyse his or her particular social characteristics, and those of his or her immediate social system, in order to grasp the variety of social resources and rules of conduct available (Whittington 1992). Managers can thereby free themselves from exclusive reliance on the capitalist resources of ownership and hierarchy, and open up the political resources of the state, the network resources of ethnicity or, if male, the patriarchal resources of masculinity. Sociologically sensitized, managers can also play reflexively on the ideological resources of their profession – exploit the Classical apparatus of strategic management not just for its technical answers but also for the enhanced legitimacy won by glossy display. The value of a MBA can lie in its packaging as much as its content. As for competitors, no presumptions should be made about their strategies without analysis of their social as well as industry structures. In planning moves and counter-moves, Systemically aware managers will not assume that competitor logics are the same as their own. In international competition in particular, competitors' political power may be as important as their market power.

To conclude, the Systemic perspective challenges the universality of any single model of strategy. The objectives of strategy and the modes of strategy-making depend on the strategists' social characteristics and the social context within which they operate. From this perspective, the Classical approach emerges as culturally highly specific – after all, it originated in just two large American companies, Du Pont and General Motors, controlled by a single family during the 1920s. It may work well in certain contexts, and often the appearances at least of Classical rationality may be required anyway, but it will not translate everywhere. To insist on a socially alien form of strategy-making – whether in a Japanese *keiretsu* or a patriotic American business – is to court disaster. Moreover, to assume that your competitors or customers operate according to the same model of strategy as yourself risks substantial strategic miscalculation. A state-backed Chinese enterprise or a growth-oriented managerially controlled firm will not respond to competitive signals in the same way as a Classically run business; and, in any stand-off with an Anglo-Saxon profit-maximizer, both are likely to hold out much longer. The main message of the Systemic perspective, then, is that strategy must be sociologically sensitive.

Conclusions

The four approaches to strategy introduced in this chapter differ widely in their advice to management. The Classical school confidently prescribes a rational, detached and sequential approach, offered as a universal norm. The Evolutionary and Processual perspectives are more cautious, each sceptical of strategists' capacity to direct strategy effectively in this rational hierarchical way. For Evolutionists, environmental change is typically too fast, too unpredictable and too implacable to anticipate and pre-empt; their advice is to concentrate on day-to-day viability while trying to keep options open. Processualists doubt whether either organizations or markets work with the ruthless efficiency that Classicists and Evolutionists respectively claim, and incline therefore towards patient strategies of incremental adjustment and cultivation of core competences. Finally, Systemic theorists take a more relativistic stance, insisting that both the ends and means of strategy depend on the character of prevailing social systems, and that therefore even the hyper-rationality of the Classical school may be appropriate in some social contexts – but only some.

The main characteristics of the four approaches are summed up in Table 2.2. For the Classical school, strategy should be formal and explicit, its objective unambiguous profit maximization. Evolutionists generally agree on the second part – for high profitability is essential to survival – but regard efforts to secure this through extravagant long-term strategies as so much futile distraction. Efficiency is the Evolutionists' watchword. Processual theorists too dismiss Classical formality, seeing strategy as 'crafted', its goals vague and any logic often only emerging in retrospect. But where Processualists find economic irrationality, Systemic analysts search for other rationalities: for them, modes of strategy are deeply embedded in particular social systems, and their processes and objectives may be perfectly rational according to the criteria of the locally dominant groups.

The main focus of each of these approaches varies accordingly. For the Classical school, success or failure is determined internally, through the quality of managerial planning, analysis and calculation. The Processualists are inward-looking too, concerned with political bargaining processes, the adjustment of managerial cognitive biases and the building of core skills and competences. The two other approaches emphasize the external. Evolutionists stress the determining impact of markets, and the Darwinian processes of natural selection. Systemic theorists argue that, to understand what is really going on within the organization and amongst competitors, the strategist must be sociologically sensitive.

Table 2.2 also associates each approach with the particular decades of their emergence (cf. Mintzberg *et al.* 1998). The Classical approach, with its emphasis on planning and analysis, had its heyday in the 1960s, a time of steady growth and American economic and technological confidence. Faith in planning was dented hard by the largely unforeseen oil shocks of 1974 and 1979 (Wilson 1990), leaving the field open for both the Processual stress on bounded rationality and the Evolutionary awe for market forces. Evolutionary arguments gained still greater resonance with the popularity of free-market economics during the 1980s.

The most recent arrival is the Systemic approach to strategy. Although firms have always differed in their objectives and contexts, the closing of the twentieth century and the opening of the new have forced a sharper appreciation of difference. The end to the stark opposition between capitalist America and the communist Soviet bloc has allowed a more nuanced appreciation of the different textures of market economies and the rich variety of their linkages with the rest of society. The former communist economies have themselves bred a wide variety of capitalisms – from the wild Mafia capitalism of Russia to the deliberate 'red capitalism' of China. The dramatic successes – and occasionally equally dramatic failures – of Asian economies have drawn attention to the very different social structures that underlie their business systems. Even in the West, privatization has brought into the economic sphere organizations that must compete, yet which also operate with complex social and economic motives and rely upon many non-market resources. The profit-maximizing entrepreneurs and competitive markets of the textbooks are not the only reality with which strategists must contend. Competitive strategy in complex environments requires a Systemic sensitivity to the diversity of contemporary economic practices.

Table 2.2 **The four perspectives on strategy**

	Classic	Processual	Evolutionary	Systemic
Strategy	Formal	Crafted	Efficient	Embedded
Rationale	Profit maximization	Vague	Survival	Local
Focus	Internal (plans)	Internal (politics/cognitions)	External (markets)	External (societies)
Processes	Analytical	Bargaining/learning	Darwinian	Social
Key influences	Economics/military	Psychology	Economics/biology	Sociology
Key authors	Chandler; Ansoff; Porter	Cyert & March; Mintzberg; Pettigrew	Hannan & Freeman; Willliamson	Granovetter; Whitley
Emergence	1960s	1970s	1980s	1990s

Guide to reading on competing theoretical approaches to strategy

The strategy discipline is finally beginning to emerge from the strait-jacket of ortho-doxy. As the world gets more complex, so should there be more differences of view.

There are two good overviews of various theoretical positions in strategy. Mintzberg *et al.* (1998) provide a lively account of ten 'Schools' of strategy thinking, more sympathetic to what they call the Learning School than the Classical Design, Planning and Positioning Schools. De Wit and Meyer (1999) may be more even-handed, analysing a series of key topics in the light of important articles that take diametrically opposed views. Two of the key topics – Strategy Formation and Organizational Purpose – are directly relevant to the two axes of Figure 2.1, but also covered are substantive issues such as globalization, networks and strategic change.

There are more specialized contrasts of perspective in the strategy field. Lowendahl and Revang (1998) provide a useful comparison of 'postmodern' approaches to strategy with Classical 'modernist' approaches. Ghoshal *et al.* (1999) offer a passionate critique of the contemporary relevance of the Classical approaches associated with Chandler and Porter. Lengnick-Hall and Wolff (1999) contrast the core logics of the capability (resource-based), guerrilla and complexity perspectives on strategy. Whittington (1996) analyses the evolving strategy field according to a different schema to that given here, emphasizing the notion of strategy as 'practice'.

Two key issues dividing the field currently are the role of planning versus emergence in strategy formation and the importance of internal resources relative to external industry position. On the first question, the lively discussions of the Honda case in Mintzberg (1996a), Goold (1996), Pascale (1996) and Rumelt (1996) provide the sharpest debate. Mair (1999) gives a sardonic and knowledgeable overview. On the second question, there is good coverage in both Teece *et al.* (1997) and Baden-Fuller and Stopford (1994), though both are inclined towards the resource-based view. Porter (1996) offers a defence and development of his external approach to positioning.

3 Strategic leadership

To be successful means to be liked, and to be liked means, in many ways, to be alike.

(Dahrendorf 1959: 46)

Introduction

The Classical literature projects the image of strategists as managerial professionals, dedicated to their firms, impersonal in their judgements and promoted on their merits. These are the expectations and attitudes embedded in every MBA degree: managerial skill and hard work can take anybody to the top.

According to Alfred Chandler (1990), during the twentieth century, it is exactly such professional top managers that have risen to leadership positions in all the major advanced economies of the West. His study of the evolution of big business in the United States, Germany and the United Kingdom from 1880 to the 1940s highlights the transition from idiosyncratic and inefficient family control to the professional and meritocractic managerial capitalism of today. At the end of the last century, the strategists were still the great industrial entrepreneurs of the history books – John D. Rockefeller of Standard Oil, Alfred Herbert in machine tools and Werner Siemens and Robert Bosch in engineering. However, the very success of this generation in building their industrial empires created the need for a new class of professional managers, able to co-ordinate and develop large-scale enterprise. Thus, at General Motors, the chaos created by founder William Durant was superseded in 1923 by the orderly systems of the great managerial practitioner and thinker Alfred Sloan. In Europe, too, professional managers such as Carl Duisberg of Bayer and Henry Tetley of Courtaulds emerged for the first time early this century. Men such as these, the consolidators and builders of twentieth-century business, are the ancestors and prototypes of the readers of this book.

Chandler's (1990) hagiography of professional management represents the mainstream of Classical thinking. This chapter, though, will focus on two different perspectives, one regarding the Chandlerian paradigm of professional management as too dull, the other dismissing it as too naive.

From the fringes of Classical theory has recently emerged a new model for top management, that of the heroic leader, whose inspired visions transcend the desiccated calculations of the humdrum professional. From the Systemic perspective, on the other hand, come accusations of managerial self-interest and social privilege. For Systemic theorists, getting to the top depends on neither merit nor heroism, but on careful conformity.

Before going on, however, we should pause for a Processual warning. Both Classicists and Systemicists are convinced that it is what top managers think and do that really matters. Processualists are not so sure. Their scepticism about deliberate hierarchical decision-making leads them to suspect a gap between strategic decision and action (Cohen *et al.* 1976). Whatever the intent of top management, a firm's actual strategy often emerges from a combination of accident and the entrenched slow-changing routines of the organization's middle (Mintzberg 1978). It is easy to exaggerate the significance of top management and to ignore the less advertised influence of middle managerial initiative or inertia. In place of the top-down Classical and Systemic models, therefore, Nonaka (1988) proposes the notion of 'middle-up-down' management.

Despite such Processual caution, American authors especially continue to promote a heroic model of leadership with few restraints. Even if occupying the wilder fringes, this leadership model has all the individualism and confidence of the Classical tradition. The advocates of 'visionary' leadership present top managers as gifted charismatics, inspiring in their visions, assured in their command. This powerful message is introduced in the next section, along with some critiques in particular from the Systemic perspective. The Systemic critique gathers force in the second section, as it focuses on the social characteristics of managerial elites, and the social interests they represent.

Visionary leadership

For today's business elite, 'leadership qualities' matter. Prominent American pundit John Kotter (1990) argues that in the turbulent fast-changing environment of the 1990s it is leadership, not just plain old management, that is required. Management is about providing the order and procedures necessary to cope with the everyday complexity of big business. Leadership, by contrast, is about coping with change. Management is important, but it is above all change that business will need to master in future years. In this perspective, Kotter (1990: 103–4) concludes: 'Most US corporations today are overmanaged and underled.'

Corporate leaders such as Steve Jobs of Apple, Jack Welch of General Electric and Jan Carlzon of SAS are lauded as exemplars for managerial imitation (Westley and Mintzberg 1989: see 'Dogged leadership, American style'). These men (and men they almost always are) have a capacity to impress on their employees inspirational 'visions' of what their organizations are for and where they are going. For Steve Jobs at Apple in 1980, the vision underpinning his strategy and guiding his people was: 'to make a contribution to the world by making tools for the mind that advance humankind' (Collins and Poras 1991: 11). Unlike financial targets, which appear simply as impositions to be satisfied, such visions provide an

Dogged leadership, American style

Al Dunlap has the classic modest origins of an American corporate hero. The son of a ship-yard worker in Hoboken, New Jersey, his only further education was at the West Point military academy. From there he became an executive officer at a nuclear-missile station in Maryland, before joining Kimberly-Clark, the pulp and paper company.

Dunlap's career progressed rapidly, with top management posts in several American companies. But his most famous appointment was as chief executive of the Scott Paper company in 1994. On his arrival, the company was losing money and facing a credit-squeeze. In just over a year, Scott was announcing record results and the company's share price had multiplied two and a half times.

In an interview with *Forbes* magazine, Dunlap put his success down to leadership. 'When you come in people are thirsting for leadership', he explained. 'You have a window of one year, and I passionately believe that at the end of one year, the window comes down like a steel door. If by then you haven't shown great leadership, dealt with the restructuring and determined what business you're in, it's over.' Leadership involves courage and charisma. Dunlap continued: 'I remember a meeting early on where I got 1700 or 1800 people together in the main office. I outlined my program, including the major job cuts. After I delivered this message, I thought: "Geez, how am I going to get out of the door without being mugged?" But as I left, people clapped'.

The job cuts were major indeed. Dunlap fired 11 000 people, one third of the workforce. Nine out of the top eleven executives went as well. So too did the former Chief Morale Officer. The headquarters was sold and 70 per cent of its staff made redundant. Dunlap acquired the nick-name 'Chain-saw Al'.

But a good leader should not be afraid of unpopularity. As Dunlap told *Forbes*: 'If you want somebody to like you, get a dog. I've got two; I hedged'.

In 1998, Dunlap's next big turnaround, at Sunbeam, went disastrously wrong. There were accusations of accountancy fraud and Sunbeam's share price collapsed to a quarter of its level on Dunlap's arrival. Chain-saw Al was fired.

Sources: *Forbes*, 28 August 1995; *Fortune*, 20 July 1998.

enduring sense of purpose, a continuing source of motivation. Steve Jobs commented: 'I don't feel that I'll ever be done. There are lots of hurdles out there, and there's always a hurdle that I'll never reach in my lifetime. The point is to keep working toward it' (Collins and Poras 1991: 10).

As well as providing direction, strategic vision can endow the corporate leader with extraordinary power: 'Visionary leadership inspires the impossible – fiction becomes truth' (Westley and Mintzberg 1989: 31). The visionary leader can triumph over the most adverse circumstances. Without irony, Bass (1985: 17–18) even cites the decisive impact of Lenin's revolutionary leadership in 1917, as told by Leon Trotsky, as a model for the modern manager of today. Lenin led a successful Communist Revolution in a primitive precapitalist society. Trotsky believed that it was the sheer persuasiveness and determination of this one individual that allowed the Revolution to prevail, even though all the social and economic conditions

---

Alan Sugar's vision statement

In 1987, Alan Sugar, the entrepreneur who had risen from his impoverished origins in the East End of London to build the consumer electronics giant Amstrad, explained his strategic vision to an audience at City University Business School, London. He also cocked a snook at the pretentious statements of more established companies. He said: 'Pan Am takes good care of you. Marks and Spencers loves you. Securicor cares. At Amstrad, we want your money.

Source: *Financial Times*, 30 April 1987

---

of contemporary Russia were against it. In other words, a single leader can turn the tide of history.

This power comes from leaders' alleged capacity to inspire and motivate their followers in a way no mere 'manager' can do. 'Visionary leadership creates drama; it turns work into play' (Westley and Mintzberg 1989: 31). For followers, leadership visions are felt not as externally imposed targets but as something that is their own. Appealing to Freudian transference theory, Kets de Vries (1988) argues that the power of leaders comes from their ability to satisfy human psychological needs. Our readiness to identify with leaders' objectives, and to exert ourselves on behalf of their purposes, is attributed to a human reluctance to face the responsibilities of selfhood and a search therefore for the authority of someone else. Releasing us from unresolved internal conflicts, leaders are able to unleash our energies onto their own external objectives.

Leadership capacity, then, is a valuable resource. Who are the leaders, and how can they be made? Bass (1990) identifies the characteristics of the 'charismatic' leader as including self-confidence, self-determination, eloquence, energy, expressive behaviour and personal insight. How can we acquire these characteristics? The original usage of 'charisma' implies qualities that are literally God-given, something rather beyond the scope of normal management theory. But Bass (1990) is resolutely democratic. According to him, we can all develop these leadership qualities if only we get exposure to appropriate career experiences and training in the relevant skills. Moreover, these leadership qualities can be learned and applied at every level of the organization. We do not need to wait for divine inspiration; management development schemes can make us all charismatics.

With their emphasis on clear direction, individualism and performance, the advocates of visionary leadership come broadly within the Classical tradition of strategy theory. But the Classical tradition is not always comfortable with these pushy bedfellows. Visionary leaders cannot quite be relied on in either objectives or methods. Their visions can turn too easily into 'magnificent obsessions', remote from the humdrum duty of profit maximization (Noel 1989) – witness the grandiose political ambitions of Robert Maxwell, embracing the Soviet Union, the British Labour Party and Israel. Their strategy implementation is often rather eccentric. Moses was a great prophet, but it took him forty years to lead his people from Egypt to the Promised Land; a proper manager would have taken only forty days (Czarniawska-Joerges and Wolff 1991).

The complexity of contemporary organizations has caused some within the Classical tradition to qualify the more rampantly individualist models of visionary leadership. The business biographies on which they draw put too much focus on the personal qualities of particular leaders and exaggerate the powers of a single individual. Leadership stories contain a good measure of self-advertisement. Thus Nadler and Tushman (1990) warn that charisma on its own is rarely enough to change a large organization. Reviewing the experience of Jack Welch at General Electric, David Kearns at Xerox and other prominent role models, they conclude that such leaders

> *are important catalysts in their organizations. Their successes to date, however, are not based simply on strong personalities. Each of these executives has been able to build teams, systems and managerial processes to leverage and add substance to his vision and energy. It is this interaction of charisma, attention to systems and process, and widespread involvement at multiple levels that seems to drive large system change.*
>
> (1990: 94)

In other words, heroic leaders need pernickety followers.

Born to lead

According to some, leadership qualities are a happy fluke of personal character. According to others, they are the product of good training. For a fortunate few, at the top of some of the world's largest firms, leadership is an accident of birth.

Consider the car industry. The chairman of the world's second largest company, William Ford, is the great grandson of the Ford Motor Company's founder at the beginning of the last century. The President of Peugeot-Citroën is Pierre Peugeot, and the director for innovation and quality happens to be Robert Peugeot. Over at Volkswagen, chairman Ferdinand Piëch started his career at his family's car company, Porsche. Ratan Tata heads up Tata Sons, India's biggest business group and producer of the country's first home-designed car, the Tata Indica. At Hyundai, South Korea's largest car manufacturer, Mong-koo Chung is defying his father, the group's founder and dominant shareholder, by insisting on staying on as chairman despite pressures for corporate reform. Across the sea in Japan meanwhile, Hiroshi Okuda, the first chairman of the Toyota motor company from outside the Toyoda family, spent 2000 coping with speculation about the likely succession of 43-year old Akio Toyoda to the leadership of the world's third largest motor company. In big business, a good name still counts.

Sources: *Guardian*, 24 May 2000; *Financial Times*, 2 June 2000; *Financial Times*, 21 June 1999.

But neglect of teams and process is not the only danger of the individualistic worldviews of leadership advocates. Rather than celebrating the personal qualities of leaders, the Systemic perspective emphasizes the social characteristics of those who reach leading positions. The next section will develop this Systemic approach to business elites. First, however, in this section we conclude by considering how social and historical conditions can severely qualify the universalistic assumptions of much leadership theory.

From the Systemic perspective, the very concept of 'leadership' is inherently culture-bound. By comparison with Continental Europe or the Far East, Anglo-Saxon cultures are peculiarly individualistic, valuing autonomy and free enterprise above collective action and state interests (Wilks 1990). The individualism of the leadership ideal is therefore particularly consistent with prevailing American and English prejudices. The fascination with business leaders is not the same elsewhere in the world. There is not even an equivalent word to 'leadership' in the French language (*Le Monde* 13 October 1990: 5). Amongst the overseas Chinese, the traditional notion of paternalistic 'headship' has much more meaning than the American concept of individual leadership (Westwood 1997). Even where leadership does have some equivalent, its connotations are not the same. Thus in Germany the old 'Fuhrung' tradition of industrial leadership has become deeply unfashionable, because of its close identification with a discredited military model and its disastrous association with 'der Führer' himself (Berghahn 1987). Leadership is not something easily to be translated across cultures.

The German case warns also that leadership's allure can change according to historical context. Czarniawska-Joerges and Wolff (1991) suggest cycles of Western interest in 'leaders', 'managers' and 'entrepreneurs', with leaders just a passing fad. As Table 3.1 indicates, fascination with leaders tends to follow economic crises and ends with political crises. Thus, as the 1930s saw prolonged economic depression and growing attacks on big business, managerial theorists such as Elton Mayo and Chester Barnard countered capitalism's critics by proposing leadership as a beneficent and necessary form of authority, providing order and stability in a tumultuously divided world (Miller and O'Leary 1990). In his influential *Functions of the Executive*, Barnard (1938: 283) characterized leadership as the 'indispensable social essence . . . without which co-operation is impossible'. While Barnard was writing, Hitler, Stalin and Mussolini were all engaged in ensuring social order and co-operation under their own leadership. The 1980s, following another period of economic crisis, again produced leaders not managers – Ronald Reagan and Margaret Thatcher. Their successors are distinctly unheroic. United Kingdom Prime Minister Tony Blair and German Chancellor Gerhard Shröder pride themselves as non-ideological managers. It seems that our fascination with leadership, and leaders themselves, may rise and fall with the times.

Table 3.1 **A chronology of business elite images**

1920s	Entrepreneurs	1960s	Leaders
1929	*Economic crisis*	1968	*Political crisis*
1930s	Leaders	1970s	Managers
1939–45	*Political crisis*	1973–75	*Economic crisis*
1940s	Managers	1980s	Leaders
1950s	*Economic hope*	1990s	Entrepreneurs
	Entrepreneurs	2000s	Managers?

Source: Adapted from Czarniawska-Joerges and Wolff 1991

But some leadership characteristics hardly change at all. Table 3.2 compares the ethnic, gender and religious characteristics of the American business elite at the beginning of the twentieth century and the end. As Peter Temin (1999) shows in his analysis of the Chief Executives of Fortune 500 companies in 1996, the business elite is still almost wholly white male, and from native-born Protestant families. Despite spectacular exceptions such as Hewlett-Packard's Carly Fiorina, women in particular do not seem to have penetrated the glass ceiling. Daily *et al.* (1999) analyse the scant progress of women at the top of American business over the ten years 1987 to 1996. There were just two women serving as chief executives of Fortune 500 companies in 1996, exactly the same number as a decade before. There were eleven women serving as inside directors of Fortune 500 companies, against eight in 1987.

Table 3.2 **The American business elite (%)**

	1900s	1990s
Women	0	0
African Americans	0	0
Asian Americans	0	0
Immigrants	10	5
Catholics	7	5–10
Jews	3	2–10

Source: Temin 1999

It seems that 'leadership' is narrowly relevant even in America. The concept is a masculine one – defined in terms of men and understood in ways that exclude women (Czarniawska-Joerges and Wolff 1991). The leadership performance of women such as Margaret Thatcher appears therefore 'reminiscent of Shakespearian times, when men played all the female roles: brilliant but artificial' (Czarniawska-Joerges and Wolff 1991: 543). As a result, Rosener (1990) observes, women in senior management positions often avoid masculine leadership styles, abrasive and authoritarian. According to her research, women 'lead' by more participative, informal and subtle means, through networking and empowering.

Indeed, the whole rhetoric of leadership is highly sexualized. Calas and Smirch's (1991) reading of Henry Mintzberg's writings on managerial leadership highlights the sexual and penetrative nature of his language – the manager is portrayed as liaising, probing, infusing, potent and physical. They point also to how the word 'seduction' stems from the Latin *ducere*, to lead. Whether as power-dressers in sharp suits, or Californian entrepreneurs in tight jeans, business leaders are bent on seducing us. For Calas and Smirch, a great deal of the contemporary fascination with business leaders is homo-erotic. Leaders achieve so much because they turn us on.

In sum, leadership may be a vital and empowering force in contemporary organizations, but it remains a cultural, historical and gender-specific phenomenon. It might work for men in 1980s America; it will not necessarily work for you in other times, other places. The Systemic perspective therefore breaks with the individualistic assumptions of the leadership tradition to emphasize the social character of managerial elites. Less personal and less celebratory, the Systemic approach stresses how top management shares collective characteristics, collective interests.

Business elites

The Systemic approach shifts concern from leadership personalities to social strata. The focus is on classes, professions and societies. Entry into the business elite is not won simply by individual merit but also by social conformity. Strategies are influenced by the interests of dominant groups rather than being determined simply by the calculus of profit.

The first Systemic challenge to Classical assumptions comes over the very emergence of the modern managerial class. Celebrated by Chandler (1990) as the protagonists of efficient objective professionalism, for the managerial economists (Baumol 1959; Marris 1964; Williamson 1967) these new managers are the self-serving, empire-building parasites of a degenerate capitalism. Modern management is not professionalizing and perfecting capitalist strategy-making; it is perverting it in its own interests.

These accusations are built upon a shift in top-management characteristics that was first extensively documented by Berle and Means (1967). They noted that as large companies grew and later generations succeeded founders, the ownership of American business became more and more dispersed. Amongst the top 200 US companies in 1930, only 11 per cent were wholly or majority owned by a single individual or compact group of shareholders. In about 44 per cent of these top 200, no group of shareholders owned more than 5 per cent of the shares. As shareholders become more dispersed, they have less interest in running their companies. So diluted had shareholdings become by the 1930s, Berle and Means (1967: 102) contended, that in about half of American business 'ownership' and 'control' had become separated. American capitalism was succumbing progressively to 'managerial control'.

Chandler (1990), of course, interpreted the emergence of professional managerial control as representing progress for contemporary capitalism. Comparing with the United States and Germany, he attributes the relative stagnation of the British economy during the first half of this century to the persistence of conservative and unprofessional familial control in business. Berle and Means were more cautious in their assessment of the professional manager, asking:

> Are we to assume for him [the manager] what has been assumed in the past with regard to the owner of enterprise, that his major aim is personal profits? Or must we expect of him to seek some other end – prestige, power or the gratification of professional zeal?
>
> (1967: 114)

The suspicion of Berle and Means was that managers were no longer just concerned about profits.

Robin Marris (1964) answered Berle and Means to suggest that managerially controlled enterprises tend to maximize growth rather than profits.

Size provides shelter from hostile takeovers; it provides personal prestige and power; it tends to correlate with high salaries. Marris conceptualized the different strategic orientations of managerially and owner-controlled firms as in Figure 3.1. The curved line represents the trade-off between profitability and growth: growth is good for profits at a moderate level, but as it accelerates beyond 10 per cent it begins to damage performance. The horizontal straight line indicates the acceptable rate of profit, say 7 per cent, below which shareholder revolt or a hostile takeover is likely. According to Marris (1964), an owner will opt for the moderate growth/high profit strategy represented by point A. Left to their own devices, however, managers will go for the strategy at point B – maximizing growth within the constraint of just about acceptable profitability. Empirical studies have shown that, without an effective takeover threat or appropriate financial incentives, this growth-maximizing/profit-satisficing strategy is exactly what managers tend to do (Holl 1977; Lawriwsky 1984).

Figure 3.1 **Managerial versus owner strategies**

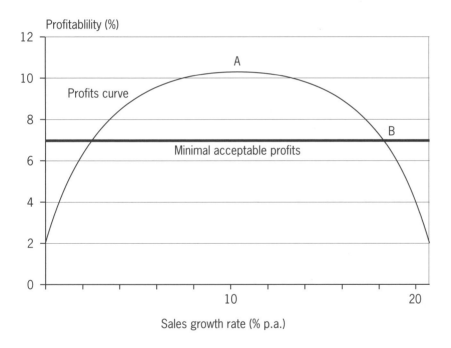

Source: Adapted from Marris 1964

Managers, however, are not all the same. Recent Systemic approaches have tended to point to the different interests and rationalities of the various professional groups within management. From a largely Processual perspective, Miles and Snow (1978) have pointed to how internal political processes can lead to the domination of a firm's top management by representatives of particular functional groups – accounting, production, marketing or research and development. The supremacy of any particular group makes a difference to strategy because managers bring the skills and

conceptual biases of their functional training to bear on strategic problems. Thus, according to Miles and Snow (1978), firms dominated by production and accounting professionals tend to be cautious, inward-looking
'defenders' in their strategic orientations, while marketing and research
and development dominated firms are characteristically 'prospectors',
more innovative and risk-taking (cf. Hambrick 1983).

Recent Systemic research has shifted the focus from the managerial
politics of individual firms to professional competition within society at
large. Within particular societies, certain professional groups may win a
prestige that gives them systematic advantages in the internal politics of
companies throughout the economy. The dominance of any individual
professional group may then bias the strategies of whole economies.
Systemic approaches suggest that Anglo-Saxon economies have become
particularly dominated by accounting and financial professionals.

Neil Fligstein's (1987, 1990) analysis of the origins of corporate presidents among the large US firms confirms the decline of founding entrepreneurs emphasized by Alfred Chandler (1990): between 1919 and 1979,
they fall from more than a quarter to less than 5 per cent of corporate presidents. However, Fligstein's analysis also demonstrates the fall of presidents
with manufacturing or sales backgrounds, against a steady rise of finance
professionals – from as little as 6.1 per cent before the Second World War
to more than a quarter in 1979 (Figure 3.2). Finance seems to have
achieved a similar pre-eminence in British industry too. Comparative
analysis of the backgrounds of European chief executives in the 1990s
shows that a fifth of British chief executives had built their careers in
finance, two and a half times more than French and German chief executives (Mayer and Whittington 1999). On the other hand, only one in ten
British chief executives had backgrounds in technical functions such as
engineering or R&D, less than half the proportions in France and Germany.

Fligstein's (1990) comparison with France, Germany and Japan, where
finance professionals are far less prominent, suggests that this financial
domination in Anglo-Saxon business does not by any means conform to a
universal capitalist logic. Armstrong (1985, 1987, 1991) argues rather that
the dominance of particular managerial professions in particular countries
is due to their competitive success against other professions in exploiting
the local opportunities of their social contexts. The success of the British
finance profession, for example, is due to the importance of auditing in an
economic system in which business has traditionally relied on external
stock market funds, by contrast with Germany and Japan, where long-term
relations with particular banks are important. Finance and accounting
professionals in Britain were strengthened still further by state intervention during two World Wars, when civil servants relied on their skills in
order to increase productivity and prevent profiteering. The merger booms
of the 1960s and 1980s gave a final boost to the profession, as financial
techniques became central to both enabling takeovers and managing the
subsequent conglomerates.

The dominance of top management positions by a particular professional group can profoundly bias corporate strategy. For Armstrong (1987),
competition between the professions for managerial ascendancy involves
the enthusiastic promotion of each profession's own technological

Figure 3.2 **Backgrounds of the presidents of the largest US corporations, 1919–79**

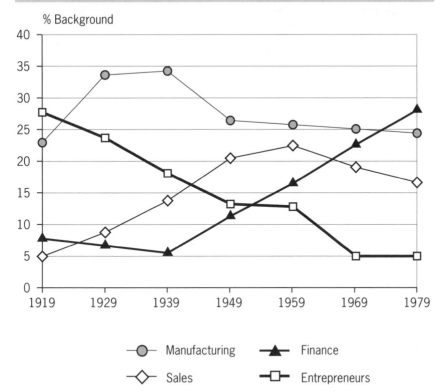

% Background

Source: Fligstein 1990

apparatus, and the systematic denigration of rival professional technologies. The success of a particular profession, then, is bought at the expense of commitment to a markedly narrow area of professional expertise. According to Armstrong (1987), the expertise of accountancy and financial professionals focuses on the extraction and distribution of profits rather than on the building of value-creating activity itself. Consequently, the professional bias of British top management is towards efficient exploitation of existing businesses, not the entrepreneurial building of new ones. Doyle (1990) makes a similar accusation: financially driven companies are too 'right-handed' – short-term, cost-focused and inward-looking. He argues that British industry needs to become more 'left-handed' – market-driven, outward-looking and innovative.

But changing a society-wide professional bias in top management is not easy. Once a profession gains advantage, the process tends to be self-reinforcing. Although originally suspected as the rickety empires of dubious tycoons, now that financially oriented conglomerates have reached such prominence, they have become quite accepted as a legitimate way of doing business. Fligstein (1987) found that once a few finance presidents had been appointed in a particular industry sector, they spread fast as rival companies imitated the new trend. As accountants rise to the top, they begin to define success in their own terms, and structure their strategies to make best use of their own skills. Consequently, the dominance of finance and accounting is established on a self-perpetuating system, only likely to be broken, according to Fligstein (1990), by economic crisis, intervention by the state and the successful definition of a new way of doing business by some other profession.

The Systemic argument, then, is that business leadership is not simply a matter of heroic high-performance individuals, but involves the collective advance of self-interested social groups – managers in general or particular professions. Often strategy is biased by managerial interests or professional technologies. Dominance by particular social groups can, moreover, influence the behaviour of whole economies. This is a controversial thesis, one that is contested even within the Systemic perspective.

For a start, the dominance of professional managers over shareholders is not complete by any means. Scott's (1990, 1992) analysis of the top 250 British companies in 1988 found that forty-one still had individuals or families able to exert control through shareholdings of around 10 per cent or more. More than half of these top companies still had very considerable concentrations of shareholdings – whether familial, corporate or state. Even amongst more diffusely owned companies, Scott (1990) argues that 'constellations of shareholders are able to join together in order to exercise a collective discipline on management'. According to Scott (1990), then, managers would be unwise to count on any revolution of control.

The presence of family interests within the firm can introduce criteria for strategic decision-making different from simple profit maximization. The owners of capital may not necessarily operate as the perfect capitalists of Classical theory. Concern to protect dynastic interests may lead family-controlled firms to low-risk strategies and a reluctance to rely on outside finance (Birley 1990). Retirement and inheritance tax requirements can also affect policy, while formal planning processes and outside professional management advice may be suspected. Whitley (1990) finds that the characteristic reliance on personal control by the owners of Chinese family business constrains them to strategies of low diversification, heavy reliance on subcontractors, and simple, direct organizational structures.

The pervasiveness of family control can have system-wide effects on economic performance. Chandler (1990: 390) blames the lingering hand of personal familial control for the relative decline of British business by comparison with the professionally managed competitors in the United States and Germany: 'in Britain, a large and stable income for the family was more of an incentive than the long-term growth of the firm'. In sum, whether or not familial control is still extensive, the logics informing strategic action in particular companies are clearly dependent on the nature of company control.

The pattern of shareholdings in a particular society also structures access to positions of business leadership. In France, where family ownership remains important, one-third of the top managers of the 200 largest French businesses in 1991 enjoyed family connections, whether as founders, inheritors or relatives (Bauer and Bertin-Mourot 1992: see 'Top managements in Europe'). Promotion in the family firm is not necessarily based simply on merit, but often on personal relationships.

Top managements in Europe

In a study of top managers in the top 200 companies in France, Germany and the United Kingdom, Michel Bauer and Benedicte Bertin-Mourot (1996) discovered some stark differences.

As indicated in Figure 3.3, in the mid 1990s, more than one in five French chief executives were either inheritors (14 per cent) or founders (eight per cent) of their companies. In Germany, 16 per cent of chief executives were either inheritors or founders. On the surface, the United Kingdom appears the most meritocratic in the origins of its chief executives – until educational background is considered. No less than 36 per cent of British chief executives had been educated at one of the top twenty public schools (Eton, Winchester, Harrow, etc.), while one third had been to Oxford or Cambridge (this 'Oxbridge' total accounts for half the chief executives with any degree at all). France has its own elites too, though recruited more competitively through examination. Just three elite higher education institutions – Ecole Polytechnique, the Ecole Nationale d'Administration and the leading business school HEC – accounted for 57 per cent of all French chief executives. These three institutions recruit about 0.01 per cent of each generation of young French people. Bauer and Bertin–Mourot were unable to trace an equivalent institutional elite in Germany. None the less, 45 per cent of the top 200 German managers held doctorates.

Figure 3.3 **Ownership backgrounds of European chief executives**

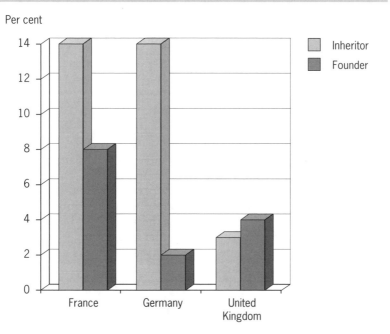

Source: Mayer and Whittington 1999.

Family advantages are not always obvious, however. Many Systemic theorists argue that family privilege and nepotism can survive unseen because it is disguised by elitist education systems. The point of elitist education systems is to exclude all but the most talented outsiders, while simultaneously legitimizing the ascent of less able insiders.

Access to the top of business in many societies is controlled through narrow educational channels. In France, more than half the presidents of the top 200 companies have issued from just three relatively small institutions, the Ecole Polytechnique (X), HEC and the Ecole National d'Administration (ENA) (Bauer and Bertin-Mourot 1996). These institutions recruit their pupils disproportionately from a small number of exclusive lycées in the wealthiest Parisian *arrondissements*. Though different in detail, the British educational system achieves a similar channelling function: one-third of top managers had studied at Oxford or Cambridge and more had attended top private schools (Hannah 1990). From the Systemic perspective, early education is critical to career success. Regardless of managerial merit and experience, the chances of reaching top management are determined long before ever entering the business world.

The business schools themselves are not quite the meritocratic institutions they might seem either. Europe's most prestigious business school, INSEAD, can fairly claim to be forming the international business elite of the future. But, as Marceau's (1989) research shows, this elite group of students is recruited largely from the children of existing social elites. One-third of Marceau's sample of INSEAD graduates were the children of business owners, company chairmen or managing directors. The rest were overwhelmingly upper middle class, almost all coming from elite educational institutions: of British INSEAD graduates, nearly two-thirds were from Oxford or Cambridge universities and 84 per cent had come from private schools. The role of an elite business school like INSEAD appears less as a channel for talent to reach the top than somewhere to give the already privileged sufficient gloss of competence to be accepted by their leap-frogged subordinates (cf. Cohen 1988).

Not only is the meritocratic vocation of the elite business schools in question. Perversely, much business school teaching may be profoundly inconsistent with the requirements of the very uppermost elite of decision-takers. Useem (1984) identifies in British and American capitalism 'an inner circle' of closely interlinked business directors. In Britain, for example, Useem found 154 directors who each sat on at least three main boards from amongst the 196 leading companies. These men were drawn substantially from the upper class – 37 per cent were members of exclusive gentlemen's clubs such as Brook's or White's and more than 20 per cent had a hereditary title. The roles of these men transcend the interests of their own particular firms to include the safeguarding of the interests of capital in general, particularly in the political sphere. As the advocates and guardians of British business as a whole, their concerns are no longer merely with the competitive advantage of individual firms. They act according to a class-wide rationality. The problem for the ambitious manager is not only that talent alone is unlikely to give access to this 'inner circle', but that even the elite business schools provide wrong preparation. Useem comments on the business school curricula:

What is not offered . . . is training in either the science or art of classwide leadership . . . . The ability to mix adeptly in the highest circles, to comprehend the cross currents of complex political environments and to serve as intermediary between the two frequently warring institutions – business and government – these are the requisite skills for which conventional schooling can offer little advanced preparation.

(1984: 103–4)

Indeed, the ruthless competitiveness and individualism promoted by some business schools may actually disqualify graduates for these classwide responsibilities.

Conclusions

The Classic 'leadership' approach offers an inspirational message. Today's business world demands an unwavering commitment to change and a clear sense of direction. Visionary leadership is the mechanism for such change, providing the ideals to shape strategy and the energy to make it happen. Leaders can give employees their sense of purpose and transform their work into play.

This is heady stuff, and not just rhetoric. No doubt characters such as Steve Jobs or Jack Welch are able, for a time, to achieve something special. But for all the celebration of particular leaders, more cautious Classical theorists still insist on the importance of the ordinary conscientious work of the employees who actually turn visions into reality. The individualistic bias of the leadership literature downplays the collective efforts that after all make an organization what it is. The leader needs his followers as much as they need him. From the Systemic perspective, this heroic individualism also obscures the social conditions for leadership. The recent Anglo-American writings on leadership do not translate easily into other cultures; they may not transfer into other periods. Many of these writings propagate an ideal to which women managers have little access. This Systemic critique has important implications for both business strategies and managerial careers.

Being a good strategist is not necessarily enough. Leadership is about more than just fitting strategy to the market environment; it is about fitting yourself to the social environment. Leadership is not equally available to all, but the privilege of particular elite groups in society. The Systemic theorists dispute still who these groups are, and the influence they have on strategy-making. The managerial economists assert the ascendency of the new managerial class, governed by the logic of growth rather than profit. Others point to the lingering importance of families in business, and the distortions their personal interests may impose on economic rationalities. Even where families do not directly control, elite education systems ensure that the children of owners have privileged access to top managerial positions. For Useem (1984), at least, even the MBA degree is not enough to open the doors of the inner circle right at the very top: for entry into the highest echelons, the MBA graduate must unlearn some of the lessons of competitive strategy and adopt the transcending class-wide rationality of the capitalist class as whole.

What does this imply for the manager ambitious to reach the highest strategic decision-making levels? The Systemic perspective suggests exactly the opposite to the heroic individualism of the visionaries. Access to leadership positions is structured by collective social characteristics – class, gender and professional. Opportunities to advance are determined by the social characteristics of those at the top. The key is to identify these and to conform. As Dahrendorf (1959) put it at the beginning, the successful are 'alike'. If you want to get to the top in Britain at least, the gloomy advice of Systemic theory is to be a male public school accountant.

4 Strategic choice

While the miser is merely a capitalist gone mad,
the capitalist is a rational miser.

(Marx 1954: 151)

Introduction

In the previous chapter we looked at who takes strategic decisions; in this chapter we consider how the decisions get made. There seems to be plenty of help here: the textbooks are full of techniques and concepts to help us make our strategic choices. Yet the confident precision and showy sophistication leave some lingering doubts. If strategic decisions were really this easy, nobody would get rich. Are the financial techniques really as helpful as all that? Does corporate planning actually work?

The Classical school answers firmly 'yes'. Financial techniques are essential to guide profit-maximizing strategic decisions. Formal planning provides the detached objectivity necessary for long-term strategic coherence. Strategies should be formulated through a deliberate process of rational analysis.

The Processualists mock Classical pretensions to rationality. For them, formal decisions rarely have the significance attributed to them: strategies emerge out of the pattern of events. The language of 'strategy formulation' carries misleading connotations of deliberate rationality; we should prefer the less presumptuous notion of strategy formation' (Mintzberg 1978). Strategies form out of a mixture of analysis and instinct, routine and spontaneity, top and bottom, fortune and error. To rely just on the formal analyses of finance and corporate planning is to detach yourself from where strategies really get made, the day-to-day operations of the organization as a whole.

Systemic theorists are inclined to accept this Processual scepticism about formal analysis, but do not come to the same conclusions. The practical failings of formal analysis are not all that important. In the context of Western business at least, planning and financial processes are useful rituals. The show of rationality, if not the substance, is essential to the maintenance of legitimacy.

Strategic investment decisions

Almost all strategic decisions involve an investment of some sort. Whether these investments are in physical assets or people, they can be represented quantitatively in the form of financial figures. For the Classicists, this reduction to the common denominator of finance is a critical step, allowing the rigorous comparison of strategic options and the unambiguous resolution of dilemmas.

Accordingly, the Classical school of strategy has evolved a number of sophisticated financial techniques for supporting the strategic decision-making process, including break-even analysis, sensitivity analysis and various investment appraisal methods based on discounted cash flows.[1] What these techniques share is an aspiration to approach strategic decisions in a structured rational manner that will finally produce a clear ranking of strategic options. The strategic option that promises the greatest net benefits, quantified in financial terms, should always be chosen. Rankings make strategic choice easy. In a sense, technique obviates decision.

Grant (1991a) argues forcefully that these rational decision-making techniques are becoming increasingly important in the contemporary business environment. As markets globalize, competitive pressure for excellence increases; as the markets for corporate control become ever more active, underperforming firms face growing threat of takeover. Concluding that firms will less and less have the luxury of being able to diverge from the goal of long-run profit maximization, Grant (1991a) contends that value-maximizing financial techniques must now guide strategy-making worldwide. Ideally, discounted cash flow calculations should be used to ensure that only strategies offering the highest net present value are chosen. If strategic investments open up new strategic opportunities in the future, these too should be included in the value analysis through option pricing techniques.[2] Grant concedes that these sophisticated financial techniques are not always feasible. However, where discounted cash flows are hard to forecast, and future options are impossible to value, he still insists on the baseline decision rule that only strategies that yield a post-tax rate of return in excess of their costs of capital should be chosen.

The normative logic of this financially driven approach to strategic decisions is attractive. In a competitive environment, survival does require close attention to economically optimal strategies. The Processual critique, however, is that organizations do not really work according to these normative ideals, nor do they really need to. In practice, all organizations and markets are so imperfect that the competitive pressure to optimize is slight. Managerial perfectionists should relax. In the complex reality of organizational life, managers who assume that strategies get chosen simply on financial criteria face certain confusion and disappointment. Effectiveness within real-world organizations requires an acknowledgement of the human frailties of their members.

Empirical studies of strategic investment decisions certainly confirm that financial techniques are much abused, even ignored. Marsh *et al.*'s (1988) case studies of strategic decision-making in three British companies found that, although each had formal capital expenditure manuals governing procedures for investment decisions, in practice these were side-lined. Finance directors did not have their manuals readily to hand and anyway dismissed them as 'out of date' or 'boring'. In their similar study, Carr *et al.* (1991) discovered one finance director whose manual prescribed a hurdle rate set eighteen years before and which had been left unadjusted despite all subsequent fluctuations in interest rates. Both Marsh *et al.* (1988) and Carr *et al.* (1991) uncovered other widespread problems in the application of financial appraisal techniques, many of them leading to a systematic underestimation of the long-term strategic benefits of particular projects. Terminal values of fixed assets were ignored; projects were assigned short and arbitrary life-spans; projects were evaluated against the *status quo* rather than the 'without investment' case; few alternatives were considered, often only one; and managers, concerned for their own jobs no doubt, revealed themselves to be very reluctant to consider the option of disinvestment. Project evaluations could even be retrospective: Carr *et al.* (1991) cite a British manufacturer's decision to adopt a focus strategy whose financial rationale was only calculated after the investment commitment had been made.

Clearly there is room for technical improvements in the actual application of financial decision-making processes. In their article 'Must finance and strategy clash?', Barwise *et al.* (1989) argue that financial calculations need not constrain strategy if only applied properly. Easy corrections to common mistakes include the calculation of projects' cash-flows over their real life span, not some standard and arbitrary period set by convention; a recognition in the base case of the likely decline of existing businesses if no investment is made, rather than the usual assumption of continuance of the *status quo*; writing into the calculation the terminal values of a project; and, most liberating, valuation of the options that a project opens up for the future, by comparison with those left closed in the absence of any action. This notion of strategy involving 'real options', unlike the conservatism of standard discounted cash flows, positively promotes innovation and experimentation (see 'Betting on the future'). According to Barwise and his colleagues, finance and the long-run need not clash.

Betting on the future

Options borrow some of the fatalism of Evolutionary theory and apply it to the purposes of Classical planning.

A financial option contract conveys the right, but not the obligation, to purchase some particular asset in the future at a pre-set price. In the same way, a 'real option' keeps open the possibility of making a strategic move at some time in the future, at some cost today. In situations of acute uncertainty, when it is hard to know where the future will lie, it often makes sense to keep alive as many real options as possible, while minimizing the costs of each. Using similar probability techniques to those in financial option pricing, the costs and possible benefits of options can be precisely calculated and entered into the strategic plan.

In the jargon of evolutionary theory, those who like to hold lots of low cost options are called r-strategists; those who invest all their resources in a very limited range of options are K-strategists. Fish, with their multitudinous spawn, are r-strategists; human beings, with their small families, are K-strategists. Neither approach is necessarily better than the other: the strategist should switch from one strategy to another according to the environment and its uncertainty.

A classic switch from r-strategy to K-strategy was that of Nokia in the 1990s. Founded in the mid nineteenth century, by the early 1980s Nokia had lost its way, with interests in mature commodities such as paper, chemicals and tires. The company spent the next decade casting around for new opportunities, with acquisitions and new ventures in televisions, VCRs, and computing. One fortunate investment was the purchase in 1991 of the British mobile phone manufacturer Technophone. As mobile phones took off, Nokia quickly divested itself of its other activities. Within a decade and a half, the company had transformed itself from mature conglomerate into the world's largest mobile phone company.

Sources: McGrath 1999; Sorenson 2000; *International Management*, July/August 1992.

But the hardline Processualists are not reassured by such promises of technical reform. They suggest that these financial techniques are based on fundamental misunderstandings of what decision-making is really about in organizations. In practice, strategic decision-making criteria need not be reduced to a single financial variable and decisions anyway may not have the importance that Classicists attribute to them.

Whatever the potential of discounted cash flow techniques to resolve the dilemmas between the long and the short term, high risk and low risk, profit maximization remains an ambiguous criterion for many managers. In their classic study of directors in twenty-one large British companies, Norburn and Grinyer (1973–4) found consensus in nineteen of them that profit was the number one objective. But they could discover little internal agreement amongst colleagues on how profitability was actually measured – whether by profit margin, return on capital, share price or whatever. Senior managers were equally vague in assessing other objectives. Norburn and Grinyer (1973–4) found that amongst their twenty-one firms the median number of strategic objectives stated by various directors was six, but that the median number of objectives stated in common by more than half of any directorial team was only one. The authors recall how in one company, where the seventeen primary strategic objectives were inscribed on the wall of the boardroom, just one director succeeded in remembering them all, while his colleagues could only agree on the existence of three. Similar studies (Bourgeois 1980; Dess 1987) have found equal ambiguity amongst American top management teams. Intriguingly, Bourgeois (1980) established a negative correlation between goal consensus and financial performance: the implication is that managers only agree on strategic goals when forced to by deteriorating financial performance.

It seems, then, that senior decision-making teams are remarkably tolerant of ambiguity, formulating their strategies according to often vague and even contradictory criteria. Net present value is too stringently precise for them. This relaxed approach to decision-making criteria is possible, according to radical Processualists, in part because 'decisions' do not have the significance we usually attribute to them.

Decisions are often not 'taken' but 'happen'. Cohen *et al.* (1972) suggest that moments of decision occur when four independent streams happen to coincide: 'problems', 'solutions', 'participants' and 'choice opportunities'. Problems demand attention; solutions are answers looking for problems; participants are the constantly varying crowd of organizational actors carrying different problems and solutions; and choice opportunities are occasions when organizations are expected to make decisions. According to Cohen and his colleagues, organizations are like 'garbage cans' into which these four independent elements are thrown together and shaken until a more or less random conjunction produces a decision. Thus a board meeting is a choice opportunity whose decisions depend on the problems and solutions its particular participants happen to bring. When the Chairman repeats golf club gossip that a related company is for sale, he is introducing a solution looking for a problem. When the marketing director next reports low sales growth, she provides a problem for the solution: a decision to expand by acquisition gets made.

This 'garbage can' view of decision-making in practice as the outcome of near chance collisions between problems and solutions certainly helps account for the limited search for alternatives found typically by the studies of Carr *et al.* (1991), Marsh *et al.* (1988) and Hickson *et al.* (1986). But even this anarchic view of the decision process may exaggerate the status of decisions in strategy formation. In understanding organizational strategy, Mintzberg and Waters (1990) provocatively suggest that decisions 'get in the way'.

Mintzberg and Waters (1990) point out that we conventionally assume that decisions represent commitments to future actions. However, as honest recollection of our own good resolutions would confirm, decisions in practice are often followed by no actions, or even by quite different actions from those we intended. Conversely, actions are not necessarily the outcome of any identifiable single moment of decision. As Mintzberg's (1978) analysis of escalating American commitment to the Vietnam War suggests, events often take on their own momentum, with decisions only flickering on the surface. It would be hard to say whether the President of the United States – supposedly the most powerful man in the world and certainly surrounded by highly intelligent and informed policy advisers – ever really decided to commit 600,000 men to the doomed defence of a corrupt regime, but that, somehow, is what happened. In the grand unrolling of events, decisions can appear almost irrelevant (see 'Mission Creep in Mogadishu').

Mission Creep in Mogadishu

In 1992, President George Bush committed 30,000 American troops to Operation Restore Hope, a six week mercy mission to bring food to the starving people of Somalia. Welcomed on the beaches by representatives of the feuding Somali warlords, Secretary of State Laurence Eagleburger was confident 'that we were going to do something very precise and limited and then get out'.

> But the mission to supply food soon expanded. First, the influx of foreign aid disrupted local power structures based on the control of scarce resources. Second, the United States felt unable simply to pull out leaving nothing changed except a temporary stock of food. Backed by the United Nations, the Americans became sucked into a process of 'nation-building' – the building of physical and civilian infrastructure necessary to get Somalia back on its feet. And this inevitably got them involved in local politics. The new President Bill Clinton determined to disarm the Somali factions and, in particular, launched a fatal hunt for the most powerful warlord, General Mohamed Aideed. Unfortunately, the forces sent out to Somalia for food distribution and nation-building were not well suited to this new mission. In October 1993, fifteen lightly-armed US Rangers searching for Aideed were massacred in the Somali capital of Mogadishu. More casualties followed. In response to a massive outcry at home, the Americans rapidly cut down their commitment and handed over responsibilities to other UN forces. The last US troops left Somalia in 1995.
>
> US and UN interventions have been governed since Somalia by the 'Mogadishu line' – the fear of stepping beyond a certain point after which escalating commitment and inappropriate resources set off an irreversible slide to failure. This fear of 'mission creep' kept the United Nations out of Rwanda during the massacres of 1994 and semi-detached through the Balkan civil wars of the 1990s.
>
> Sources: Clarke and Herbst 1996; *Time*, 18 October 1993.

A great deal of our behaviour is not 'decided' at all. The best top managers may be the ones who take fewest conscious decisions. Nelson and Winter (1982) suggest that as strategic decision-takers gain experience they build up strategic 'routines' by which to guide their responses to the various challenges that regularly crop up in their industry. The more expert they become, the more they can rely on their established routines and the fewer real decisions they need make. For Nelson and Winter, good strategists are like experienced divers, who keep their legs straight automatically. A conscious decision would only disrupt the smooth action of the dive.

The ways in which 'decisions' can get spread over time, as in Mogadishu and Vietnam, or in which they become gradually submerged in routines, as in diving, lead Pettigrew (1990) to recommend a different vocabulary for thinking about strategy formation. Rather than focusing on strategic 'choice', with its connotations of deliberate decision, he prefers to talk simply of strategic 'change', which carries no assumptions about the process. *Change* lifts strategy formation above particular moments or episodes of decision to considering processes extending over time. *Change* conveys the sense that strategy formation involves more than the analytical procedures of decision, but demands also the uncertain and grinding tasks of implementation. Choice on its own is too easy.

Why, when formal decisions are so often irrelevant and top decision-makers are merely surfing on the waves of fortune, do we invest them with such importance? According to Brunsson (1989), decision episodes are about a great deal more than just determining what to do. Decision episodes are also about mobilizing support and creating commitment. Thus decision-making processes are often designed not to produce rapid action but to build consensus and momentum – as, for example, the Japanese *wa* process, involving the exhaustive passing round of decisions between colleagues (McMillan 1985). 'Decisions' are also necessary for allocating responsibility: for someone to take the credit, or evade the blame, it helps after the event if some kind of formal decision was recorded. Finally, decisions are valuable in themselves irrespective of the actions that follow. The vigorous display of decision-making activity – the setting up of committees or working parties – can even substitute for action. Vociferous talk and profuse announcements actually serve to legitimate inaction.

A deeper Systemic point can be made about decisions in our society. March and Olsen (1989: 50) suggest that 'The idea of intelligent choice is a central idea of modern ideology . . . . Decision activities are part of a set of rituals behind which a society assures itself that human existence is built around choice.' In other words, we cling to our particular ideals about decisions because they are central to our notion of human dignity.[3] The managerial commitment to decisions as distinct and consequential episodes, and continuing faith in the need for analysis to substantiate them, merely reflect the prevailing norms of Western culture.

In this culture, Brunsson (1989) argues, contemporary organizations need to produce more than just 'products' in order to survive; they must also generate 'legitimacy'. Organizations are required to conduct themselves 'along lines that are generally regarded as reasonable, fair, efficient, rational, modern and so on' (Brunsson 1989: 4). These norms of reasonable conduct are constructed and enforced by the stockbrokers' analysts, management consultants, financial journalists and business schools who together form the 'institutional environment' in which business operates. If a firm ignores these institutional expectations it risks acquiring the damaging labels of eccentric, old-fashioned, unreliable, a bad employer and worse. Appearances as well as performance matter to survival.

In this sense, formal decisions and financial calculations are necessary rituals to demonstrate conformity to local cultural expectations. Discounted cash flow procedures are not followed because they provide optimizing solutions, but for the sake of appearances. To complain that these procedures are ineptly applied is to miss the point: what matters is that the formalities have been observed. As the Systemic perspective illuminates, the financial rituals of decision-making vary widely by time and culture.

Thus H. Johnson and Kaplan (1987) argue that the contemporary American obsession with financial calculation is a local phenomenon contingent on the rise of the multidivisional firm. Until early this century, management accounting was engineering driven, based on measures of 'conversion costs' – for example, stock-turn or labour hours per unit. These measures were designed to motivate and evaluate the efficiency of internal processes, not to calculate profit *per se*. However, from the 1920s onwards, newly diversified firms such as Du Pont and General Motors developed and disseminated financially driven measures, such as return on investment, in order to measure on an equal basis the performance of the various different kinds of business in their portfolios. Quarterly financial reporting requirements began to displace accounting measures of internal efficiency. It became possible for managers to run their businesses 'by the numbers'. As understanding a set of ratios became as important as knowing about the actual processes of production, financial professionals replaced engineers at the top of business. Strategic decision-makers relied more and more on financial calculations because that was all they knew.

But the Systemic perspective shows that this American logic of financial calculation is not universal. Carr and Tomkins (1998) compared the relative weights of different factors, financial and otherwise, for strategic decision-making amongst American, British, German and Japanese vehicle components manufacturers. Their analysis of Strategic Investment Decisions (SIDs) in these companies suggested that financial calculations were particularly important for the American and British companies (see Table 4.1). Considerations of implications for relationships with partners up and down the value chain were critical to the German and Japanese manufacturers. The British were outstanding for the poor quality of strategic analysis behind their decisions. Typical pay-back periods varied widely too: in the United Kingdom, just over three years; in the United States four years; in Germany, five years and in Japan five and a half years. In an earlier study, Carr *et al.* (1991) quote a German chief executive who deliberately extends required pay-back periods on risky projects to allow for experimentation and failure. Financial logic, of course, would require that he should shorten pay-backs to include an enhanced risk premium. But, as the German manager said, he was in business, not banking.

Table 4.1 **Contrasting calculations in strategic investment decisions (SIDs)**

Relative weights %	Financial analysis	Value chain	Cost drivers	Competitive strategy	Other
14 US SIDs	42	9	3	46	0
26 UK SIDs	46	24	6	17	7
25 German SIDs	15	44	7	31	3
13 Japanese SIDs	15	53	3	29	3

Source: Carr and Tomkins 1998.

The Japanese indeed have a completely different approach to the role of figures in strategy and management (see 'Accounting for the Japanese'). The electronics giant NEC never uses discounted cash flow, while Toyota calculates cash flows but refuses to use them as a decision principle (Williams *et al.* 1991a). Japanese corporate strategies seem guided by grand sweeping statements of ambition, rather than narrow financial criteria. Thus Komatsu declares its strategic intent as simply to 'encircle Caterpillar', while Canon's mission is 'beat Xerox' (Hamel and Prahalad 1989). These declarations can fuel strategic passions which appear as the height of financial irresponsibility. Thus when Honda was overtaken by Yamaha as Japan's number one motorbike manufacturer, the company responded by declaring: 'Yamaha so tsubu su!' ('We will crush, squash and slaughter Yamaha!'). There followed a stream of no less than eighty-one new product launches in eighteen months. This massive effort nearly bankrupted the company, but in the end left Honda as top dog once more (Abegglen and Stalk 1985; Collins and Poras 1991).

Accounting for the Japanese

Unlike in American business, where management accounting is concerned with controlling deviations from budgets, accounting in Japan is designed to ensure effective behaviour in the first place.

Williams *et al.* (1991b) report three Japanese motor industry press-shops where accounting measures are presented in physical terms – thus labour costs are translated into number of press strokes per hour. These simple physical measures focus workers on readily understandable means to productivity improvements. Another common technique is Functional Cost Analysis. Here every element of a product is expressed as a verb: for instance, a pen has primary function to 'make marks', and subsidiary functions to 'flow ink', to 'store ink', to 'prevent stains'. Each function is attributed a value in the eyes of customers and the target cost for the product is set in line with the sum of the functional values (Yoshikawa *et al.* 1995).

Overall, Japanese accounting follows an 'influencing' rather than 'informing' rationale. The point is to influence managers and workers to contribute continuously to strategic objectives rather than to tell top managers retrospectively when they are not. Hiromoto (1988) gives two examples from Hitachi. At one video cassette recorder plant, overheads continue to be allocated between departments according to direct labour costs: top management knows this is inaccurate, but this form of allocation drives behaviour consistent with Hitachi's objective of increased automation. At Hitachi's refrigeration plant, on the other hand, overheads are allocated according to the number of product models: this time, the point is to reinforce trends towards modularization and standardization of parts. In other words, financial measures are used to underpin the strategy, not just to police employees.

Recalling Marx (1954), it seems that neither the Germans nor the Japanese are 'rational misers'. Perhaps the Anglo-Saxons are 'capitalists gone mad'. Anglo-Saxon business culture appears peculiarly driven by financial simplicities. We invest decisions with greater significance than they really have because of our cultural expectations of rationality. We clothe this rationality with the logic of finance because of the institutional dominance of financial professionals.

The Processualists taunt that, in practice, criteria are too vague, decisions too complicated and people too fallible to rely on financial techniques. But the Systemic manager working within the context of Anglo-Saxon big business should not be too dismissive. The technical failings of financial calculation do not matter so much. The rigmaroles of finance are still useful because they produce legitimacy. In this institutional environment, it pays to at least go through the motions of financial calculation.

Corporate planning

The Classicists themselves recognize some of the limitations and biases to which purely financial decision-support techniques are liable. Since the 1960s, various corporate planning techniques have emerged alongside, most famously SWOT analysis, the Boston Consulting Group's portfolio, the General Electric Screen, the experience curve and Michael Porter's five forces analysis.[4] Though they are less quantitative in orientation, these various techniques share the Classical aspiration to rational decision-taking, and retain profit potential as the underlying criterion. Moreover, they can provide a basis for a more comprehensive and long-term analysis than the iterative comparison of successive investment projects. For Hax and Majluf (1990), planning techniques introduce a qualitative element complementary to the quantitative bias of financial calculations of net present value (NPV). They advise (1990: 92): 'before using NPV calculations first consider the overall attractiveness of the industry and the strength of the business unit in order to understand the investment decision'.

Indeed, the very origins of contemporary corporate planning came in part as a reaction against excessive financial bias. The great pioneer of corporate planning was General Electric, under the leadership of chief executive Fred Borsch during the 1960s and early 1970s (Pascale 1991). A marketeer in a company previously dominated by finance, Borsch felt the need for a new approach to managing the vast, diversified and stagnant conglomerate that General Electric had become. During his office, General Electric collaborated with the McKinsey Consulting Group to develop the industry attractiveness-business strength matrix (the General Electric Screen), with the Boston Consulting Group to work on the experience curve and with the Harvard Business School to establish PIMS (Profit Impact Market Strategy) analysis. By the early 1970s, these approaches were implemented and co-ordinated by a large central corporate planning department, the prototype of those which spread throughout Western business during the decade. Borsch's successor, Reginald Jones, allowed central planning to grow to over 200 professional staff.

But General Electric's corporate planning structures became prone to exactly the sclerosis that the Processualists warn of. Pascale (1991: 199) relates how computers were spewing out daily reports twelve feet high on individual businesses. General Electric had not solved its problem of slow growth and was hard hit by the recession of the early 1980s. A new chief executive, Jack Welch, instituted a massive rationalization throughout the corporation, becoming known as 'Neutron Jack' after the bomb that eliminates people but leaves buildings standing. Chief victim of the rationalization was the over-elaborate corporate planning system. Welch provided an epigraph:

> We had constructed over the years a management apparatus that was right for its time, the toast of the business schools. Divisions, strategic business units, groups, sectors, all were designed to make meticulous, calculated decisions and move them smoothly forward and upward. This system produced highly polished work. It was right for the seventies . . . a growing handicap in the early eighties . . . and it will be a ticket to the boneyard in the nineties.

(Pascale 1991: 213)

Bye, Mr. Porter?

Michael Porter first came to fame with *Competitive Strategy* (1980), in which he introduced his 'five forces' approach to industry structure analysis. Profit potential was supposed to be decided by the interplay of buyer power, supplier power, competitive rivalry, threat of new entry and threat of substitutes. The task of strategists was to place their assets in industries that were structurally favourable.

All this expressed a typically Classical approach to strategy. Profit potential could be calculated according to objective criteria. The world was sufficiently stable that today's industry structure could predict the future's. Strategy was about plotting favourable positions on the battlefield of business and simply moving assets around by remote control.

The resource-based view, of course, sees profit potential as determined by unique and valuable resources held internally to the firm, not simple positions in external industries. In a large-scale empirical study, Rumelt (1991) has famously shown that industry factors typically explained 9–16 per cent of variations in profit, against 44–46 per cent for firm-specific (business unit) factors. Rumelt (1991) concluded that industry didn't matter very much. This resource-based reasoning has been extended by Teece *et al.*'s (1997) argument for 'dynamic capabilities'. Industries are moving too fast, boundaries are too fluid, for traditional industry structure to apply. What matters now is not just given resources, but the ability to continually upgrade and develop them – making resources *dynamic*.

Industry structure is not dead. Even in its high-tech sector, Microsoft proved able to defend its monopolistic control of the world's software industry for a decade and a half at least. McGahan and Porter (1997) have shown in a further empirical analysis that industry influences on profit vary widely by industry, but overall may account for a substantially larger amount than allowed for by Rumelt (1991), especially in services. In a lively defence, Porter (1996) has warned resource-based theorists that good positioning still matters, and that too great an internal focus can easily degenerate into mere obsession with operations.

The new century may be an even less hospitable place for formal planning in the Classical mode (see 'Bye, Mr. Porter?'). Boundaries are too easy to cross for traditional industry structure analysis (Sampler 1998). Intuit's Quicken instantly puts the software firm in the role of financial adviser; airlines such as Easyjet can use Internet technology to leap-frog travel agents and go direct to customers. National barriers are no obstacle either – Amazon.com suddenly competes with local booksellers world-wide (Downes and Mui 1998). In a weightless economy where brains matter more than brawn, harnessing the intelligence of employees on the ground becomes critical to strategy, not top-down command (Moran and Ghoshal 1999). As products become more complex and knowledge-intensive, the Processualists argue that it will be constant adaptive innovation rather than remote and inflexible plans that will win the day. The guerrilla tactics of Linux, not the plodding strategies of Microsoft, becomes the new model (see 'Linus and Goliath').

In his fierce critique, *The Rise and Fall of Strategic Planning*, Henry Mintzberg (1994) identifies three fundamental fallacies in Classical strategic planning. First, there is the Fallacy of Predetermination: the vain hope that planners can produce accurate forecasts. What they do, in fact, is produce a false sense of security that condemns its believers to certain surprise. Then there is the Fallacy of Detachment: the claim of professional planners that they bring objectivity and perspective in place of politics and myopia. In practice, detachment means an ignorance of the marketplace that always puts the customer second and an indifference to the product that makes it too easy to give in whenever the going gets tough. Finally there is the Fallacy of Formalization: the belief that innovation and difference are generated by analysis and structure. Actually, Classical planning has too much reason, not enough passion and intuition. The targets of formal planning are constraining by their very reasonableness. What is really needed is 'strategy as stretch', broad strategic intents that inspire companies and their employees to perform and innovate beyond the norm (Hamel and Prahalad 1994).

Linus and Goliath

Software giant Microsoft has a formal strategic planning process based on regular committee meetings and a three year plan. Three years is what it has traditionally taken to develop a major software system. Steve Ballmer, company President and responsible for planning, is adamant that there is no need to shorten horizons or flex the process: 'The fact of the matter is, the notion that everything changes every day, that customers really want a new release every three months – that's hogwash' (Cusumano and Yoffie 1998: 69).

Linux offers a different model of software – and strategy – development. Invented in 1991 as a hobby by Linus Torvalds, a 21-year-old computer science student at Helsinki University, Linux has from the first been freely available over the net. Programmers have always been encouraged to download the software and use it, test it and modify it as they saw fit. Very quickly, a Linux community of thousands emerged, dedicated to the constant, incremental improvement of the system. Improvements are offered over the net for free, even by commercial companies selling Linux support: the principle is that if you give something, you get lots more back. Nobody owns Linux; nobody controls it; nobody plans its future. It just evolves. Linux accounted for 25 per cent of the 5.4 million server operating systems shipped in 1999 (*Computer Dealer News* 7 April 2000).

In 1998, Linus Torvalds gave this account in an interview:

Seven years ago, I had no visions at all. It was fairly accidental, the development. It wasn't meant to be a big, professional operating system. It was more meant to be [for] my own personal enjoyment and my own personal use. I didn't envision it as a common desktop environment,

> *[but] more of an environment for people who happened to be interested in how operating systems worked [and] really wanted to tinker. I'm still doing just the operating system part... I'm not all that concerned about the direction myself. I don't have any goals in that sense . . . . It's still just a hobby – a big hobby.*
>
> (www.computerworld.com/more).

Supporters of Classical Planning respond by statistically testing the performance consequences of formal planning for firms. Research results are not conclusive. Boyd (1991), pooling data from several studies in order to get sufficiently large sample sizes, finds a slightly positive overall relationship between planning and profitability on most measures. But he also reports several studies with negative results. Brews and Hunt (1999) studied the practices and performance of more than 600 firms to conclude that it's all about 'learning to plan and planning to learn'. Performance benefits to planning came only after several years' experience. Sound planning provides the framework in which the kinds of incremental adjustments so passionately advocated by Mintzberg (1994) can effectively be made.

Some Processualists respond that the Classical eagerness to demonstrate direct performance benefits to planning slightly misses the point. The process of strategic planning can be as important as the outcome. Langley (1988, 1991) and Oakes *et al.* (1998) have studied the various roles of strategizing in Canadian voluntary and public sector organizations. In the first place, the planning process did succeed in collecting and analysing data about critical strategic issues. But the process was about much more than this. Planning brought three further kinds of benefit – control, public relations and, not least, 'group therapy'.

In Langley's (1991) hospital case, for instance, the extraction of information and subjection to a plan provided a means for finally bringing free-wheeling and secretive physicians under control – not by direct control, but by setting up a process to gather information and incorporating it into a structure that appeared rational and legitimate. There were more subtle control effects. In the museum sector, Oakes *et al.* (1998) found that the very process of involving curators and archivists in the construction of strategy led them to internalize new objectives for their organizations that top managers would have been hard-pressed to impose directly. Old concerns about historical integrity were insidiously supplanted by a new discourse of target markets, competition and revenue. But much planning activity is therapeutic also. In the museums, planning meetings gave managers a chance to rehearse and grow comfortable with their new language. The exchange of views and various debates in Langley's (1991) organizations were very protracted, but, however inefficient they may have looked, they did serve to release tensions, strengthen camaraderie and build consensus. Finally, adopting the language of planning looks good. In the Canadian museums, one manager acknowledged that it was 'very important to us to have these business plans to be credible to business people'. At one of Langley's (1988: 45) cases, a manager admitted frankly: 'planning was done merely to present a certain image to the government.

It was decided what image was required and a text was invented to go along with it and some figures were put on it'. Planning was pure public relations. But, however useless this planning process might have seemed in terms of actions, as Brunsson (1989) would remind us, it was still vital to satisfying the normative expectations of critical elements within the institutional environment.

Langley's (1991) conclusion is that it may not matter all that much if planning comes out with the 'wrong' answers as long as the planning process is allowed to fulfil control, social and symbolic functions that otherwise the organization might fail to achieve. The complaint at General Electric was that planning processes involved what Feldman and March (1981) have termed 'a conspicuous overconsumption' of information. The key word here is 'conspicuous'. In an institutional environment valuing quantification and rationality, the planning process, however expensive in time and effort, may be a necessary sacrifice to cultural expectations. The planning process serves both to persuade subordinates internally that a particular policy has been chosen carefully and to demonstrate to key audiences outside – shareholders or regulators – that the organization is a proper corporate citizen. In this sense, corporate planning should be seen, even if not heard.

However, Systemic analysts point out that not all societies value the forms of rational corporate planning equally. Horovitz's (1980) study of formality and centralization in fifty-two matched companies in France, Britain and Germany found quite wide differences in practice. Formal long-range planning, stretching over five-year time periods, was most developed in Britain. In Germany, planning was widespread but less formal, less long-ranging and more focused on operational issues. Planning in France emerged as little developed, and again focused on the operational. Reid and Schlegelmilch's (1990) Anglo-German comparison of planning in the mechanical engineering industry found the British ten times as obsessed about return on investment measures, 50 per cent more concerned about control and significantly more regular in their demands for reporting.

Across the Atlantic, Harvard Business School scholar Robert Hayes (1985) characterizes the typical American corporation as similarly obsessed with formal, quantified planning. In his terms, Americans use plans as detailed 'road-maps', to be followed closely; they regard competition as a matter of 'grand strategy'; for them, competitive advantage is to be seized with the 'strategic leaps' of the hare. By comparison, Hayes characterizes the Germans and the Japanese as 'tortoises', steady and sure; rather than road-maps, they prefer strategic 'compasses' that give them a sense of direction but still allow for flexibility along the way; for them, competition is a matter of continuous remorseless 'guerilla warfare'.

For Hayes (1985), the American faith in corporate planning is due to the influence of business schools and their MBA graduates. Tricked out with the latest techniques, instead of embued with deep understanding of specific technologies and industries, MBA professionals resort to the remote and formal methods of planning. Planning techniques give MBAs and consultants a claim to relevant general expertise that can be applied in each and every industry, over the heads of those who really know their industries and whose careers are tied to the long-run development of their companies. In Germany and Japan, where MBAs are much less plentiful, planning may be less widespread but for a long time business was certainly not less successful.

From a Systemic perspective, then, the rise of planning is related to a social change in the constitution of the managerial class in America. The techniques are those of professional managers working within a financially oriented business culture. The success of the Boston Consulting Group's portfolio, for example, was dependent on an institutional environment dominated by conglomerates, infused with financial values and populated by a new breed of managers badly in need of credibility (see 'The Boston Boxes'). Planning and its technological apparatus emerge as a product of their time and place. They are not to be applied universally except with the greatest caution.

The Boston boxes

The famous market growth/market share matrix originated with the Boston Consulting Group, itself closely connected with the Harvard Business School, to serve the needs of a new kind of business. This technique was first developed for the diversified Mead Paper Corporation in the late 1960s, then engaged in an aggressive takeover binge and incorporating no less than forty-five operating divisions (Morrison and Wensley 1991). The technique spread rapidly amongst other burgeoning conglomerates of the day, so that by 1972, only two years after its first publication by the Boston Consulting Group, it was being used by over a hundred major American companies.

The reasons for the wildfire success of the 'Boston Boxes are manifold. It was simple, visual, well marketed and, of course, did represent important strategic variables.[5] However, it was also peculiarly well suited to its institutional environment and the interests of dominant professional groups. Not only did the Boxes serve a new kind of clientele, the acquisitive conglomerate, but they also matched the contemporary financial language of business. As Espeland and Hirsch (1990) notice, the 'portfolio planning' idea explicitly appropriates the language and techniques of investment analysts: indeed, early versions of the matrix labelled the Boxes 'sweepstakes', 'savings accounts', 'bonds' and 'mortgages' (Morrison and Wensley 1991). Smart managers, like smart investors, were urged to spread risk by diversifying corporate assets just as investors diversify their capital through share portfolios. In this sense, the Boston model redefined the corporation as a bundle of liquid assets rather than a concrete collection of factories and people.

For the new breed of managers running these conglomerates – for whom credibility in the eyes of the stock market was essential to the funding of the next acquisition – the capacity to dress up their strategies in appropriate language was essential. The Boxes endowed adventurous and novel strategies with the legitimacy of finance and the prestige of the business schools. Internally as well, this managerial technology served to impress: 'Many corporate officers felt that in portfolio planning they had found the means to add value to their businesses and thereby maintain their authority and esteem' (Morrison and Wensley 1991: 12). Authority and esteem may have been won independently of value.

Conclusions

For the Classical approach, strategic choice is about rational profit-oriented decisions. To guide these decisions, it has developed a powerful array of financial and planning techniques. No doubt these can be helpful, but logic suggests that there must be something more to strategic choice than just plugging in the techniques. There is no competitive advantage to be had from using the same techniques as everybody else.

The Processualists are even stronger. If the information we use is inherently limited and our judgement is inescapably biased, then to trust heavily in formal analyses is to risk making grand mistakes. Strategies are best crafted in a continuous 'middle-up-down' incremental process. In practice, decisions are often not decisive; strategies emerge undecided. The detached and formal analyses of finance and corporate planning can dangerously distract from how strategies really get made. The Processual advice then is not to over-invest in rationality and to keep close to the action.

This is not to say that finance and planning are useless. As Langley (1991) argued, just the process of getting people together for the ostensible purpose of planning can have positive, if unintended, spin-offs. Systemic theorists add a more cynical view. In the context of Anglo-Saxon big business, we need planning and finance to rationalize our strategic choices because these are what the dominant professional groups and cultural norms demand. The Systemic advice is to use the techniques for the sake of credibility. In organizational politics, the ritual display of formal analysis will reassure superiors and impress subordinates. We plan and calculate to keep up appearances.

5 Growth strategies

The problem of industrial organization has puzzled me ever since I was issued my first M-16 in the army, upon which was stamped 'Made by General Motors'.

(Walker 1988: 377)

Introduction

How is it that General Motors got into making M-16 rifles for Vietnam? How and why do firms grow in the way they do? The four basic approaches to strategy offer very different answers: typically, Classicists see initiative, Evolutionists efficiency, Processualists emergence and Systemicists imperialism. This chapter examines the implications of the four perspectives for three growth strategies in particular – innovation, diversification and internationalization. As before, there are no easy formulae. Before entering the fray, the main protagonists in the debate can be introduced briefly as follows.

In innovation, the central controversy is between the Classicists, who view new product generation as something that must be closely directed, and the Processualists, who doubt both the capacity of markets to absorb radical technical advances and the ability of managers to control the creative, serendipitous processes of innovation in practice. As usual, the advice of the Processualists is to be modest. Over diversification, the debate is between the Classical and Evolutionary claim for its efficiency and Systemic suspicions of managerial self-interest. Neither the case for nor the case against diversification is conclusive, but there is sufficient cause for worry to warn anyone to tread very carefully. Lastly, on internationalization, Evolutionists again talk in terms of efficiency, while Classical game theorists emphasize the elaborate defence of oligopolistic privilege. Systemic critics add the caveat that strategists should never assume that their international competitors are like themselves.

Innovation

Many high-tech markets today are 'winner-takes-all' (Schapiro and Varian 1999). Technological innovation is about the battle to establish the industry standard. There is little room for the also-ran. Consider the fate of WordPerfect against Microsoft's Word; Digital and Motorola against Intel in the microprocessor business; Sony's Betamax against Matsushita's VHS. As Microsoft's Bill Gates admitted in an unguarded moment, establishing standards is a powerful weapon:

> *Why do we need standards? . . . I really shouldn't say this, but in some ways it leads, in an individual product category, to a natural monopoly: where somebody properly documents, properly trains, properly promotes a particular package and through momentum, user loyalty, reputation, sales forces and prices builds a very strong position with that product.*
>
> (Cusumano and Shelby 1996: 157)

There is a lot to play for in innovation. As Marx and Engels understood more than a century and a half ago, it creates and it destroys (see Innovation according to Karl Marx). Innovation should be at the heart of strategy.

Innovation according to Karl Marx

Internet tycoons might do well to hang the following extract from the *Communist Manifesto* on their boardroom walls. A century and a half ago, Marx and Engels (1848) identified the shortening of product life-cycles as a critical feature of modern bourgeois capitalism:

> *Constant revolution in production, uninterrupted disturbance of all social conditions, everlasting uncertainty and agitation, distinguish the bourgeois epoch from all earlier ones. All fixed, fast-frozen relations, with their train of ancient and venerable prejudices and opinions, are swept away; all new formed ones become antiquated before they can ossify. All that is solid melts into air, all that is holy is profaned, and man is at last compelled to face with sober senses his real conditions of life, and his relations with his kind.*
>
> (Marx and Engels 1972: 5)

For the dominant Classic tradition, a strong 'market orientation' is essential for successful innovation. In this view, effective innovation comes from seeking out customer needs and matching them with appropriate product or service offerings. Typical studies such as Project NewProd in Canada have found that successful product developments in manufacturing are two and a half times more likely to have been based on good marketing than failed innovations; in services, successful innovations are five times as likely to have relied on close 'product-market fit' (Cooper 1981; Cooper and Brentani 1991). Cooper and Brentani conclude that, for services as much as for manufactured goods, a strong market orientation – expressed by market research, extensive trials and responsiveness to customer needs – is vital to success in innovation. The advice, then, is to 'keep close to your customers'.

The implication of this Classical approach is simple: in leading the innovation process, the 'technology-push' of research and development departments must be replaced by the 'market-pull' of marketing. In his classic article on 'Marketing Myopia', Levitt (1960) accuses high-technology firms, dominated by engineers and scientists, of being production rather than marketing oriented in their approaches to innovation. Levitt argues that, to be effective innovators, organizations should be constantly scanning the horizons for new opportunities to satisfy their customers. To innovate well, 'the entire corporation must be viewed as a customer-creating and customer-satisfying organization' (Levitt 1960: 92). Simmonds (1986: 479) goes so far as to argue for an 'eighth paradigm' in contemporary business, in which marketing provides all the initiative and direction for innovation: 'The marketeer, in fact, holds the organizational responsibility for guiding innovation. Without marketing guidance, an organization will succeed only by luck or because other functions have themselves correctly assessed the market when shaping their actions.'

Research and development (R&D) efforts should therefore be integrated into, and even subordinated to, the marketing effort. Gupta and Wilemon's (1990, 1991) survey of marketing and R&D directors in 103 American high-tech firms found a strong consensus on the importance of R&D–marketing integration, with 80 per cent of marketing directors and 60 per cent of R&D directors believing that the need for integration had increased over the last five years. This need for greater integration is driven by shortening product life-cycles, faster product introductions and the greater demands of increasingly sophisticated consumers. Integration should be improved by more teamwork between functions, more job exchanges between the two departments and a shift in R&D's focus towards more urgent, less basic research (Hendry 1989; Gupta and Wilemon 1990). In a sense, central R&D departments need to learn to market themselves internally, in order to anticipate and meet the wants of fellow departments and divisions (Whittington 1991a).

The importance of 'market-pull' in successful innovation is now well established. The old ideal of the boffin in an ivory tower awaiting inspiration is an anachronism. Yet to leave innovation as simply a matter of satisfying customer needs is a little incomplete, even from Classic concerns with profit maximization. Innovation can be put to other uses than simply making customers happy. Insights from both Processual and Systemic perspectives suggest as well that the market-driven approach may not be the only effective, and profitable, means to innovate.

Two rogue members of the Classical tradition help correct the conventional marketeers' obsession with the customer in innovation. Both Schumpeterians and Marxians share the Classic focus on profit and control, but they come to radically different conclusions. The Schumpeterians point to the role of innovation in suppressing competition and dominating customers; Marxian approaches emphasize how new technologies can increase managerial control and reduce the cost of labour.

The Schumpeterian approach belongs to the Classical tradition in sharing the expectation that innovation processes can be manipulated deliberately to maximize profitability. The difference is that, for Schumpeterians, profits come from dominating customers, not serving them. Schumpeter (1934: 130–4) describes the innovative process as a constant search for the monopolistic profits due to the first mover. For him, innovation is less about improving competitiveness than avoiding competition. Prospects of market domination can motivate enormous investments in technological break-throughs. Thus American start-up Celera Genomics was prepared to invest $300 million and take three years of heavy losses in its race to decode the 3.5 billion chemical letters that make up human DNA. The prize would be patent control over the genes that constitute humanity. As Celera's controversial founder Craig Venter remarked: 'One hundred to three hundred of the most promising genes out of the tens of thousands in the whole human genome . . . should be enough to give us a tidy return' (*The Guardian*, 11 June 2000).

The Schumpeterian notion of monopolistic innovation can be given another twist. As well as empowering entrepreneurs, innovation – or just the threat of innovation – can be used by incumbents to beat-off potential challengers. This was the role of IBM's famous 'FUD factor' – the fear, uncertainty and doubt stirred up among customers by incremental changes in the company's dominant mainframe computer range during the 1970s (DeLamarter 1986). The technique has been refined by contemporary computer industry giants with the development of 'vaporware' – promises of new products that never come, but are sufficient in the meantime to put the competition on the back-foot (see 'The FUD factor in computing'). Again, innovation can be less about improving competitiveness, more about avoiding competition.

The FUD factor in computing

IBM pioneered the use of the FUD factor in the computer industry during the 1960s and 1970s. Innovation was carefully manipulated so that its customers were constantly in sufficient 'fear, uncertainty and doubt' to keep them locked in with the reassuring bulk of 'Big Blue', as the computer colossus was known.

One famous coup in the early 1970s was delivered against Memorex and other computer peripheral manufacturers who began to offer cheaper and better disk drives for IBM's dominant 360 and 370 series mainframe computers than the company's own. 'Big Blue' defended its lucrative peripheral market by repeatedly updating the interfaces between computer controllers and disk drives. These changes amounted to very tiny innovations. However, they were enough to force the peripheral manufacturers into an expensive game of second-guessing and constant reassurance of customers that it was worth investing in their drives before IBM made them out of date. Memorex was driven into liquidation by 1974 (DeLamarter, 1986).

Where IBM led, others have followed. In 1978, Intel, the chip company, found itself challenged by Motorola, whose new 68 000 microprocessor was better than Intel's 8086. Intel responded by launching 'Operation Crush'. Explained one senior Intel manager: 'We have to kill Motorola . . . . We have to *crush* the XXXX bastards. We're going to roll over Motorola and make sure they don't come back again'. Intel developed a one hundred page 'futures catalogue' packed with specifications and preliminary data-sheets for parts most of which had still not been designed, let alone manufactured. Head of the list was the promise of a chip capable of crunching numbers five times faster than Motorola's 68 000. No matter that many of these innovations were pie-in-the-sky: Motorola couldn't respond. Intel established a dominance of the microprocessor market two decades long (Jackson 1998).

While Schumpeterian accounts emphasize the control of markets, Marxian approaches focus on the control of labour. According to Marx (1954), the challenge for the early capitalists was how to break the grip of skilled craft-workers over traditional production. Organized in highly secretive guilds, literally called 'mysteries', these craft-workers were able to control the pace, organization and quality of their work, immune from the intervention of outsider capitalists. Their control was based on both their exclusive knowledge of the necessary processes and their ownership of the tools of production. For Marx (1954: 454–7), the point of the capitalist technologies unleashed by the Industrial Revolution was their power to supersede the exclusive skills and traditional tools of the old crafts.

During the twentieth century too, new technologies have been introduced to de-skill or circumvent powerful groups of workers. Noble (1977) describes how numerically controlled machine tools were developed first with US Air Force support in order to reduce the power of the strongly trades-unionized machinists to disrupt production at Boeing and General Electric during the Cold War. Under numerical control, complex machining sequences could be designed and stored on tapes held in drawing offices, rather than being left in the minds of skilled machinists on the shopfloor. At the beginning of the 1980s, after a decade of disruption by the powerful Professional Air Traffic Controllers Organization (PATCO), the Federal Aviation Administration in the United States developed computerized 'flow control' procedures for regulating air traffic on major routes (Shaiken 1985). In 1981, the new Reagan Administration provoked a strike and, able to keep 75 per cent of traffic flying with the aid of the new technology, smashed the union. PATCO strikers were removed from picket-lines in chains.

Marxians and Schumpeterians thus provide extra angles on innovation strategy. The Marxian insight is that innovation can improve profits not just by satisfying customers but also by controlling workers. As well as getting closer to customers, managers need to get closer to the shopfloor. The Schumpeterian advice is not to compete to serve customers but to deny customers competition. Customers should not necessarily be soothed and reassured: on the example of IBM and its FUD factor, it may sometimes be best to disconcert them. In short, customer-oriented R&D may not always be the most effective basis for innovation strategy.

Further scepticism about the superiority of purely customer-oriented R&D comes from more Systemic perspectives. Recalling Chapter 3, the managerial professions can be seen as in constant competition amongst themselves for leadership within the large corporations of today. The marketing profession is a late entrant to these leadership stakes, and more insecure than the financial and scientific professions because it lacks a strong base in a structured examination system. Within this context of professional competition, many of marketing's claims appear as the rhetoric of a profession seeking legitimacy and advance (Whittington and Whipp 1992). When Levitt (1960) and Simmonds (1986) argue for the supremacy of marketing in the innovation process, we need to remember that they are prominent marketeers themselves – they are the ideologues of a profession on the make. Customer-oriented R&D is at least as much in the interests of the marketing profession as in those of shareholders.

This Systemic scepticism about marketing is reinforced by the cultural specificity of the marketeers' approach to innovation. In Germany and Japan, the urgent desire to assert marketing's special interests and perspectives over those of R&D rings strange. In these economies, it is normal for managers to progress through a wide range of functions, rather than to advance through specialized professional career tracks (Petroni 1983; Nonaka and Takeuchi 1995). Marketeers will typically have worked in R&D and might do so again. The separation of the two functions is naturally blurred. The result is that, rather than marketing imposing a 'strategy' upon R&D, research is seen as at the origin of the firm's strategic capability. Technology and knowledge creation are seen as at the heart of strategy, not just its instrument.

For the Japanese (Nonaka and Takeuchi 1995; Nonaka *et al.* 2000), the Anglo-Saxon tendency to characterize the innovation process as a contest of control between marketing and technology is a reflection of typical Western patterns of rational thought. The West is too prone to seek clear and exclusive categories; the Japanese prefer the tacit and holistic. Nonaka and Takeuchi (1995) relate the tortuous history of Mitsubishi and Caterpillar's joint venture to design and build a new global line of hydraulic shovels. The Japanese were shocked to find that, in the American company, product design and specification were driven by marketing and that the designers rarely visited the manufacturing plants or talked to users. Caterpillar's processes were underpinned by a philosophy of clearly separate roles and responsibilities through which tasks were logically sequenced. Mitsubishi, on the other hand, emphasized a philosophy of 'actual experience-ism', an insistence on hands-on design and close interaction between all functions. It is not that the Japanese approach was perfect: they were forced by the inquiring American engineers to learn how to justify and document their decisions explicitly. The Systemic point is that Anglo-Saxon textbook presumptions of rational, sequential processes are not widely shared. Blind adhesion to these kinds of processes will lead to trouble when working with other cultures.

Indeed, the Processual perspective doubts whether innovation can be managed and manipulated to maximum advantage even in the West (cf. Scarbrorough and Corbett 1992: 153–4). By their very nature, R&D activities are highly uncertain: R&D invents a future that cannot be known today. Processual theorists stress both the unpredictability of innovation and the rigidities embedded in the creative process.

According to the Processualists, the market-oriented approach to innovation misleads because it overstates the predictability of markets and underestimates the complexity of organizations. As Brownlie (1987) points out, especially for breakthrough innovations, the market can provide little reliable guide to success. When IBM launched its first main-frame computers in 1952, market research had established a world market of just fifty machines (Gilder 1988). When, in 1982, it launched its first personal computers, IBM predicted a market of 300,000 worldwide; a decade later, the installed base was 110 million (Tate 1991). The market deceives because consumers' perceptions of their needs are too restricted to the familiar; consumers are ill-equipped to articulate needs when they do not know what is technically feasible anyway; and, with consumers always shifting and innovation processes often lengthy, consumer needs may well have changed by the time a specified product actually reaches the market (Brownlie 1987). Small wonder that Dr Edwin Land, holder of 500 patents, inventor of instant photography and founder of the Polaroid Corporation, despised market research (Quinn 1991).

Processualists warn too that innovation can be over-managed. Sometimes innovation comes in defiance of management. ICI only discovered polythene, a crucial packaging good, as a result of an accidental explosion in ICI's laboratories in 1933 (Reader 1975). All that was left amongst the ruins of the scientific apparatus was a small deposit of this unknown waxy substance. Further experiments were banned for safety reasons, and it was only when three scientists repeated the experiment two years later, secretly and out of hours, that the company realized they had something of value. The company's analysis, however, led them to believe that the future market was in insulating electrical cables: they had no inkling of the future boom markets in consumer packaging. More than half a century later, crucial innovations are still emerging despite, rather than because, of management. In the account of its inventor, Tim Berners-Lee, the World Wide Web too was created through a process of guerrilla innovation (see: 'If you want to revolutionize capitalism, don't tell your boss').

The Processual conclusion is that innovation is a more or less uncontrollable process, sometimes the better for the absence of management. Quinn (1985: 82), in his study of innovation in large American, Japanese and European companies, found that 'few, if any, major innovations result from highly structured planning systems'. The best way to innovate is by incrementalism, pluralism and decentralization – 'chaos within guidelines' (Quinn 1985: 83).

If you want to revolutionize capitalism, don't tell your boss

Tim Berners-Lee joined CERN – the huge particle physics laboratory in Geneva – in 1984 as a young software engineer working on 'data acquisition and control'. With a mass of experiments being performed by transient, polyglot physicists from all over Europe, often bringing their own computers and software, Berners-Lee saw a need to capture results in a common and easily accessible format. The Internet had already opened up the possibility of computers talking to each other, but there was no guarantee that they would be able to understand all the different languages and there was no common place where information could persist beyond particular interactions. Berners-Lee conceived of the World Wide Web as a place for information to sit, permanently and accessible to all.

Of course, CERN did not want something that would revolutionize the world economy. It just wanted a better library system. In March 1989 Berners-Lee put forward a proposal. There was no response. In May 1990, he put forward the same proposal, just with a new date. Again, no response. Berners-Lee continued to work on his idea but needed to get approval. After all, in his words: 'I was not employed by CERN to create the Web. At any point, someone higher-up could have questioned how I was spending my time and . . . my informal project could have ended'. Berners-Lee finally decided to launch the Web under the guise of an internal telephone directory. CERN said yes.

There was, of course, the question of what to call the new system. Berners-Lee thought of calling it The Information Mine, but feared the acronym – TIM – might sound a bit egocentric. When he hit upon the name World Wide Web, his friends all laughed. The acronym www had nine syllables, three times longer than what it stood for. It would never catch-on . . .

Source: Berners-Lee 1999.

Processualists also accuse the market-oriented approach to innovation of overestimating the flexibility of organizations and markets. Organizational capabilities and perceptions of opportunity are in practice highly sticky, tending to become fixed in particular tracks. Dosi (1988) points to the prevalence of 'technological paradigms', institutionalized sets of understandings and capacities in an industry that constrain what is seen as feasible and set competitors on shared, self-reinforcing 'technological trajectories'. The search for new ideas in industry is not an uninhibited quest for new technological opportunities, but circumscribed and guided by the established exemplars and heuristics of the sector's paradigm. Even with the revolutionary changes from manual typewriters to computerized word-processing, we still persist with the nineteenth-century QWERTY keyboard because it requires too great a leap for us to adopt the more effective ones that have since been developed (see 'QWERTY's grip').

QWERTY's grip

David (1985) tells how the QWERTY keyboard – named after the characters in the top-left line – was originally designed in the mid-nineteenth century to minimize the clash of successive mechanical keystrokes. It was amended slightly in 1873 by the Remington typewriter manufacturer to ensure that all the letters necessary for the word 'typewriter' were on one line, so allowing impressively rapid typing demonstrations by their sales staff.

Far more efficient keyboard layouts have since been developed – the 1880s 'Ideal' keyboard put all the most common characters on the same row, while during the war the US Navy introduced the Dvorak layout which improved speeds by 20 per cent and is now the system on which typewriting speed records are won. Yet still QWERTY survives. The existing stock of keyboards and trained typists has become too great to allow displacement by a better layout. Thus the word-processors of today use an inefficient system originating in nineteenth-century mechanical constraints and a Remington company sales ploy.

Once established, 'technological trajectories' are extremely hard to break out of. The momentum of developments in nuclear power stations illustrates the fixity of these trajectories. Nuclear power can be generated by light-water, heavy-water, gas-cooled or sodium-cooled reactors, but certain types of reactor predominate in particular countries according to the trajectories initiated at the beginnings of their respective industries. Thus European countries use a variety of technologies, while the United States is dominated completely by light-water reactors. The reason for this is that the first nuclear-powered submarine, USS *Nautilus*, launched in 1954, happened to use light-water technology. The experience gained from the Nautilus, and the personal investments of nuclear engineers and politicians in this technology, combined to ensure that light-water reactors got 'locked-in' and all other technologies got shut out (Arthur 1989). Since the 1950s, the institutional, engineering and political structures have not existed in the United States to support major programmes in alternative nuclear technologies, and anyone would be foolish to attempt them, even though they may be technologically at least equivalent.

The lesson of QWERTY and nuclear power is that effective innovators may not necessarily search for the absolutely superior technology, but rather work within the institutionalized paradigms of their industry. Being technically right – as the inventors of efficient keyboard layouts have been – may actually prove very expensive if implementation requires the uprooting of established mental and physical infrastructures. The Processual warning is that to pursue the optimal is to risk being too clever by half.

Not only may the boundless search for optimal technology be ill-advised, so too can be obsessive pursuit of customer need. Levitt (1960) asked the famous question 'What business are we in?', and answered in terms of the external markets served. According to him, Amtrak should have seen itself as in the booming transport business, not simply the declining railway sector. Levitt assumes that, having perceived the opportunity, Amtrak could easily have assembled the necessary managerial and material resources to have entered the related air and bus markets. But the Processualists stress the stickiness of organizational resources, and so ask a different question: 'What sort of business are we?'

Grant (1991b), in his 'resource-based theory of competitive advantage', insists that human and technological assets cannot be effortlessly reshuffled to maximize market position, and that therefore opportunities need to be defined in terms of the existing internal capacities of organizations. From this view, effective technical innovation does not come simply from scanning the external environment for market opportunities, as Levitt (1960) argues, but from looking inside to establish and build on the core competences of the organization. Thus, in Grant's (1991b) account, the successful innovation record of Canon is based on a unique, durable and self-reinforcing set of human and material resources that together form a core competence in the integration of optical, microelectronic and precision-mechanical technologies. It is by working from this core technological competence, rather than by fickle chasing after markets, that Canon has been able to serve both consumer and business needs with a succession of innovative camera, copier and facsimile products.

For the Processualists, therefore, the Classical faith in the manageability of innovation and the targeting of markets can be dangerously deluding. Accident and conservatism are enduring features of organizational life and attempts to defy this reality invite failure. Investment in innovation may not even pay. The PIMS studies of American business found that both the proportion of new products in a company's portfolio and the level of R&D spending as a percentage of sales were slightly negatively related to average profitability (Buzzell and Gale 1987). In a similar vein, Mueller's (1987) study of 551 large American companies between the 1950s and 1970s discovered that companies with a high patenting activity relative to competitors also tended to do worse than average on profits, though again the relationship was slight. Whereas the Classicists may see these low returns to patenting and R&D as a challenge to better management, for the Processualists they are clear confirmation of the uncertain, uncontrollable nature of innovation.

Diversification, integration and takeovers

The corporations which today we take for granted – whether General Electric, Fiat or Hyundai – are still novelties in the history of business. Not only are they larger than any enterprise ever before, they also combine widely different kinds of business under single ownership. The Industrial Revolution of the West was achieved largely by single businesses, concentrating their enterprise and innovation on just one sphere of operations. It has only been in the twentieth century, and especially in the post-war period, that today's highly diversified conglomerates have arisen – hence Walker's (1988) puzzle of the General Motors M-16.

In the 1950s, most large firms had been undiversified, with around two thirds of companies having more than 30 per cent of their turnover concentrated in a single area of core business (Dyas and Thanheiser 1976). By the 1990s, however, the overwhelming majority of large firms in the advanced economies were diversified (Mayer and Whittington 1999). In France, the proportion of firms with no core business accounting for as much as 30 per cent of total turnover was 65 per cent. In Germany, the proportion of such diversified firms was 79 per cent. In the United Kingdom, the figure was 84 per cent. For all the talk of focusing and return to core competences during the late twentieth century, big business continued to be diverse.

Systemic theorists suspect that this trend to diversification reflects managerial empire-building, facilitated by the peculiar facility of mergers and acquisitions in Anglo-Saxon financial markets. For Classical and Evolutionary perspectives, however, diversification is a perfectly logical development, ensuring the rational and efficient use of resources. Classical approaches put more emphasis on diversification as the outcome of rational strategic decisions, while Evolutionists just accept diversified corporations as the efficient survivors of the natural selection mechanisms of the market, remaining agnostic about whether they stumbled on their successful strategies deliberately or not. In practice, the two approaches substantially agree, sharing great reliance on the transaction cost economics of Oliver Williamson (1985) (see 'The economics of transactions').

The economics of transactions

For Williamson (1975, 1985), the extent to which firms integrate different activities under their direct ownership reflects the comparative transaction costs of 'markets' and 'hierarchies'. All transactions between people – whether buying and selling or commanding and obeying – involve certain costs. These transaction costs are raised by the bounded rationality and self-seeking opportunism inherent in human nature. Sometimes we make mistakes, sometimes we cheat. Activities will be integrated under direct ownership where it is cheaper to prevent errors and cheating by the bureaucratic methods of hierarchy. Managing activities through the open market, on the other hand, will be most appropriate where unreliable and opportunistic behaviour can best be controlled by buying in from competitive independent contractors.

According to Williamson (1985), therefore, vertical integration simply reflects the superior efficiency of hierarchies over markets in organizing the various transactions involved in the chain of distribution and supply. Horizontal integration – or diversification into parallel businesses – takes advantage of hierarchies in managing synergies and capital transfers between the elements of a corporate portfolio.

Transaction cost economics gives strikingly different recommendations about organizational scope to the resource-based view. In the resource-based view, firms should only do for themselves activities for which they have distinctive competences – the rest they should sub-contract. Transaction cost economics, on the other hand, encourages firms to keep in-house activities for which they are vulnerable to mistakes or bad-faith (Williamson 1999). Distrust, rather than competence, determines the boundaries of the firm.

Thus Alfred Chandler (1977, 1990) explains the origins of big business in late nineteenth-century and early twentieth-century America in terms of firms' need to maximize resource utilization through economies of scope and to minimize the transaction costs entailed by ever more complex chains of supply and distribution. For example, when American Tobacco introduced mass-production Bonsack cigarette-making machines, it found itself obliged to integrate both backwards and forwards. Simple market transactions would have been too unreliable for the new scale of operations. Backward integration into buying, storing and curing tobacco was essential to secure supplies on a sufficient and regular enough scale to feed the voraciously productive Bonsack machines; forward integration into distribution and marketing was necessary to ensure a steady off-take in the market and prevent any rapid accumulation of stocks. On the other hand, economies of scope were important to explaining General Motor's diversification strategy during the Depression of the 1930s. Then the need to utilize resources to their maximum drove General Motors to redeploy its spare automobile-making capacity and skills in the manufacture of diesel locomotives, domestic appliances, tractors and aeroplanes.

General Motors' 1930s diversification involved exploiting the scope economies of physical assets in related manufacturing areas. But economies of scope can even be applied to explaining the rise of the unrelated conglomerate in the last few decades. Teece (1982) emphasizes the economies of scope in intangible assets such as knowledge, learning and experience, which can be applied to a range of situations but yet are hard to trade and nearly impossible to price in open markets. Diversification therefore arises from the need to internalize the transfer and application of these intangible assets within the same ownership structure, rather than attempting to trade them on the market. Given imperfect capital markets, the skill which conglomerates are able to apply to a range of situations is the identification and exploitation of new business opportunities, whether related or unrelated. Because it is hard to transmit credibly and without loss through opportunistic buyers in the market-place, firms apply this knowledge themselves through direct conglomerate diversification. In Williamsonian (1985) terms, conglomerates arise on account of their superiority to markets in the efficient transacting of knowledge about business opportunities.

The advice of Classical and Evolutionary theorists of big business, therefore, is to look closely at existing assets and activities, and to ask what they really add to each other. Are the transaction costs of keeping particular activities in-house really lower than subcontracting them onto the open market? If not, disintegrate. Are there underutilized resources – managers, plant, channels or brands – which could be stretched to gain economies of scope? If so, diversify.

For many Systemic theorists, however, this economic rationale for contemporary big business sounds suspiciously like a whitewash. If Chandler (1977) and Teece (1982) are to be believed, the creation of huge multinational, multibusiness corporations emerges as simply the result of the unselfish pursuit of efficiency. There are grounds for scepticism. As Perrow (1981) notes, in Chandler's account all talk of profit is avoided, the term 'efficiency' always being preferred. Chandler may be indulging in some ideological sleight of hand here, but this would not matter to business decision-makers if it did not obscure the different ways in which profit can be made through diversification. For example, during the 1930s and 1940s, General Motors also diversified into electric tram transit systems in forty-five major American cities (including New York and Los Angeles). It is not obvious what extra efficiency General Motors was able to extract. What the world's largest manufacturer of cars and buses could do, however, was extend its markets by cutting back the public transit services under its control and replacing trains by buses (Du Boff and Herman 1980). Thus diversification, either vertically or horizontally, can provide profits through exploiting market power as well as simple 'efficiency'.

Classical proponents of diversification may be uncomfortable with the profits obtainable from market power, but none the less insist that in the long run diversifiers must be gaining some performance benefits if they manage to survive. Thus Chandler, while admitting that simple efficiency may not always be the spur to diversification, resorts to the Evolutionary defence:

> *Whatever the initial motivation for its investment in new operating units, the modern industrial enterprise has rarely continued to grow or maintain*

its competitive position over an extended period of time *unless the addition of new units . . . has actually permitted its managerial hierarchy to reduce costs, to improve functional efficiency in marketing and purchasing as well as production, to improve existing products or processes and to develop new ones, and to allocate resources to meet the challenges and opportunities of ever changing technologies and markets.*

(1990: 17; emphasis in the original)

In other words, existing patterns of diversification must be efficient – or, *pace* Perrow (1981), profitable at least – otherwise these large corporations would not be around any longer.

The trouble is, the typical make-up of large corporations still differs widely between countries. From a Systemic perspective, it looks unlikely that there is one universal rule of economic efficiency dictating diversification according to simple transaction costs. This is particularly the case with the conglomerate – businesses diversified into a range of unrelated businesses (such as television, domestic appliances, plastics and finance in the case of General Electric). As Figure 5.1 indicates, the rise of conglomerates in Europe is both an uneven and a recent phenomenon. The varied pattern of conglomeratization across countries seems to demand a more complex explanation than just economics.

Figure 5.1 **Conglomerates in post-war European industry: proportion of domestic top 100 firms with more than 30 per cent of turnover in unrelated business**

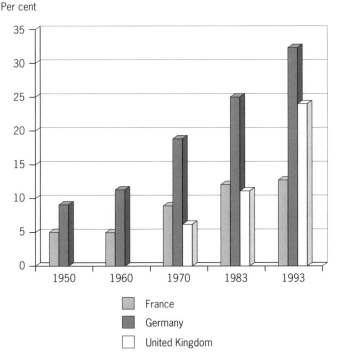

Source: Whittington and Mayer (2001);
NB no data available for United Kingdom, 1950–60.

In the Anglo-Saxon economies, the rise of the conglomerate seems to have been driven by peculiar social and institutional factors – particularly the development of capital markets in which the assembly, and disassembly, of large corporations is a relatively easy way of making a quick buck. Sociologists trace the origins of the conglomerate in the United States to the emergence of deal-driven consultants and investment banks, increasingly easy access to capital and a widespread reconceptualization of the firm as simply a portfolio of investment opportunities, rather than as an organization with an integrity and identity of its own (Davis *et al.* 1994; Stearns and Allan 1996). Thus the great 1980s merger wave took-off when two new social phenomena were added to these background conditions – the permissive regime of President Reagan and the arrival of such quick-moving outsiders to the White Anglo-Saxon Protestant (WASP) establishment as Michael Milken, Carl Icahn, T. Boone Pickens, Jerome Kohlberg, Henry Kravis. These men had sufficient personal assets or connections to become movers and shakers, but none – typically Jewish or from the southern, oil-rich states of America – had sufficient stakes to gain from defending the *status quo* (Stearns and Allan 1996). In the United Kingdom too, the emergence of the conglomerate since the 1960s has been driven by a similar mix of deregulation and opportunistic entrepreneurs such as James Goldsmith and James Hanson. All started with useful advantages but had a great deal more to gain than to lose (Whittington and Mayer 2001).

Yet the conglomerate can also be the product of conservatism and insiderism. In Germany the typical conglomerate has traditionally been either an ancient family-owned sprawl, such as Röchling or Tchibo, or a federal-state controlled local colossus, such as VIAG or RWE (Whittington and Mayer 2001). These conglomerates have been happy to sacrifice profits for stability and the privileges of control. In less developed economies, on the other hand, a certain degree of control and insiderism can actually have economic benefits. As Khanna and Palepu's (1999) study of evolving conglomerates in Chile and India indicates, increased diversification over the last twenty years had made good business sense in these business environments. Diversification facilitates the development of internal markets for managerial labour in countries where management is a scarce resource; in the presence of small and poorly informed capital markets, diversification permits the efficient allocation of capital within the portfolio at least; finally, diversification gives to companies many points of leverage against governments which still have multifaceted and powerful roles in these economies. In these kinds of environments, profit-maximizing strategy is only possible if built upon a Systemic awareness of departures from textbook conditions.

But at least in advanced economies, there is some doubt that diversification, especially via the aggressive take-overs used in the Anglo-Saxon economies, actually pays. Reviews of a host of empirical studies (e.g. Ramanujam and Varadarajan 1989; Datta *et al.* 1991) have been inconclusive. Of eighteen studies of diversification and performance, Datta *et al.* (1991) found that six suggested a generally positive relationship between diversification and profitability, six suggested a negative relationship and six had inconsistent or statistically insignificant results. These studies did not distinguish between organic and acquisitive diversification, but the literature on mergers and takeovers specifically is even more disconcerting.

On average, acquisition seems to damage the performance of acquired firms. The problem, according to Ravenscraft and Scherer (1987), is 'control loss' – the inability of top managements to absorb and manage their growing empires. In their comprehensive study of nearly 6,000 US mergers and takeovers between 1950 and 1977, the two researchers found considerable evidence that acquisitions suffered after takeover: acquired firms suffered an average postmerger profitability decline of about half a per cent per year. One-third of all acquisitions were subsequently divested, with an average lag of about ten years (Ravenscraft and Scherer 1987). Mueller's (1985) separate study of 209 American acquisitions found that mergers may impact on market share as well as profitability: although unable to distribute blame between incompetent pre-merger management and incapable post-merger management, he found that on average acquired businesses only retained 18 per cent of their 1950 market shares in 1972, while non-acquired businesses managed to retain 88 per cent of their original share over the same period. Certainly, the troubles of Volvo with regard to its Renault merger illustrate both dangers and mixed motives (see 'The Swedish Emperor').

The Swedish emperor

In early September 1993, the Swedish vehicle group Volvo announced a merger with the French state-owned vehicle group Renault. Although Renault and the French state would be clear majority owners, Pehr Gyllenhammar, Volvo's executive chairman, would be chairman of the new combined company. Gyllenhammar would be propelled from the Scandinavian margins to a central place in the restructuring of European industry.

Gyllenhammar came from Sweden's business elite. His father had been chief executive of Skandia, Scandinavia's largest insurance company, and Gyllenhammar followed him into the same job while still in his early thirties. Gyllenhammar became executive chairman of Volvo in 1971, a company in which Skandia was a major shareholder. Gyllenhammar developed Volvo's position as a niche quality car producer and a leader in industrial vehicles. He also turned Volvo into something of a conglomerate, with interests in oil, food, engineering and pharmaceuticals. Over his long term of office, Gyllenhammar showed himself to be a charming and gregarious autocrat, whose nickname in the company was 'the emperor'. He stacked the board with friends and supporters. He did not, however, acquire substantial shares in the company – only 0.10 per cent by 1993, with a capital value of about half his annual income.

The other shareholders did not like the deal Gyllenhammar had struck with Renault on their behalf. In the six weeks following its announcement, Volvo's share-price fell against the market by 23 per cent, representing value destruction to the tune of $1.1 billion. The accusation was that Gyllenhammar had sold the company too cheap, just as Volvo's market was recovering. It also emerged that the Volvo board had not been consulted about a clause in the deal allowing the French to increase their share in the new company still further. On November 30, Skandia declared itself against the deal. On 2 December, Skandinavia's largest bank, SEB, on whose board Gyllenhammar himself served, announced itself against as well. Before the end of the day, Gyllenhammar and four fellow directors resigned.

The Renault deal was dead. It was announced that pre-existing cross-shareholdings between Renault and Volvo would be terminated and that Volvo's various stakes in diversified businesses would be disposed of. Volvo's share price responded by nearly doubling in the next four months. The company was acquired by Ford in 1999.

Sources: Bruner 1999; *Forbes*, 3 January 1994; 19 December 1994.

So much for the acquired units; what about the fate of the bidders themselves in the takeover process? Takeovers are well acknowledged to raise the value of acquired firms, benefiting targets' shareholders with bid premia on average of 20–30 per cent (Asquith 1983; Bradley *et al.* 1988; Caves 1989). But the risk is that all the potential gains of the takeover are discounted in the acquisition price. The question, then, is whether the takeover process succeeds only in bidding up the price so far that all the putative benefits of the takeover are outweighed by the cost of achieving it.

Generally, acquiring firms do enjoy small increases in their share prices upon announcements of their bids, indicating some confidence amongst investors of higher future returns (Caves 1989). However, the bidders' gains are small, and the downside risks not inconsiderable. Asquith (1983) found in his large US sample that successful bidders only enjoy an average 2–3 per cent premium, while unsuccessful bidders lose nearly 5 per cent on their share prices. Bradley *et al.* (1988), in a study of 236 US bids, add some further caveats. Bidders in contested bids, whether successful or not, generally experience negative returns, especially in the case of late entrants (e.g. 'white-knights') in the bid battle. In contrast with the usual overall pattern, Bradley and his colleagues found that bidders of all kinds suffered negative average returns in the period 1980–4, a time when the relaxed regulatory regime and the enthusiasm of the investment bankers created excessive competition between bidding firms for available targets.

It is not by any means clear, therefore, that takeovers increase the wealth of bidding firms' shareholders. Morck *et al.* (1990) suspect that managerial interests motivate many bids, especially of growing and unrelated targets. Their American study found that, in the period 1980–7, bidders' share prices suffered on average a 4 per cent drop in the case of non-related acquisitions, against a 3 per cent premium for bidders going for related diversification. Bidders' values also suffered when they bought rapidly growing firms. Morck *et al.* (1990) conclude that managers were buying new businesses and new growth opportunities in order to defend or expand their personal empires – even when, on average, these were damaging shareholders' wealth.

Thus the Classical and Evolutionary claim that integration and diversification strategies must be of direct benefit to shareholders – otherwise, they would not persist – finds only the most equivocal support. Some kinds of acquisitive strategies, in particular unrelated diversification or white-knight interventions, come definitely at the shareholders' expense. But the Evolutionary theorists have a second line of defence. An active 'market for corporate control' benefits shareholders indirectly by increasing competition between managerial teams for the managing of their assets. Jensen and Ruback (1983) argue that the takeover market creates a managerial beauty contest in which shareholders can choose between rival managerial teams for control over their companies. In having the opportunity to decide whether to back or oppose various takeover bids, shareholders are able to select whichever they believe is the most promising managerial team. This market for corporate control, therefore, provides a natural selection process by which only managers maximizing shareholders' interests are able to continue in control of substantial assets.

This Evolutionary argument in favour of the indirect benefits to shareholders of an active takeover market relies on managers playing by the rules. Unfortunately, just as managers may push takeovers out of self-aggrandisement, so may they resist them for their own reasons. Takeover is likely to be followed by widespread purging of established managerial ranks and a substantial cut in strategic autonomy. Recent decades have therefore seen a proliferation of devices to help protect firms from takeover: for instance, shark-repellants (introducing restrictions on ownership transfer into corporate charters) and poison-pills (giving existing shareholders such valuable rights in the event of takeover that any bid would be prohibitively expensive) (Davies 1991).

Some of these anti-takeover devices may actually serve shareholders' interests, to the extent that they raise predators' bidding prices for their assets. But if they deter predators from making bids at all, then they restrict shareholders' ability to choose the best managerial teams for themselves. The verdict of the market is generally negative – American studies tend to report a 1–2 per cent fall in stock prices following the announcement of anti-takeover devices (Jarrell and Poulsen 1987). Shareholders clearly interpret these managerial devices as attempts to buck the market for corporate control.

In sum, the evidence does not yet allow us to judge clearly whether diversification and acquisitions are generally driven by managerial self-interest, as the Systemic critics allege, or by the unselfish pursuit of efficiency, as Classicists and Evolutionists claim. But there is enough uncertainty at least to give pause for thought. The conclusion must be to treat any proposal for diversification or acquisition with the greatest scepticism.

Internationalization

The world economy is steadily internationalizing. Between 1980 and 1999, annual world exports more than trebled to a total value of $55 600 billion (International Monetary Fund 2000). Foreign direct investment multiplied more than ten times over the two decades, reaching $566 billion by 1998 (Miyake and Thomsen 2000). The forces behind this rising internationalization are varied and much disputed.

FDI – the direct ownership of foreign activities – is a form of integration but with a spatial element. Thus one route to explaining the growth of international operations is the Evolutionary perspective associated with Oliver Williamson's (1985) 'transactions costs' approach. Here the 'internalization' of multinational activities within one enterprise is presented as an efficient response to international market failures. A less sanguine approach comes from the economics of oligopolistic competition, in which internationalization is driven by the defence or expansion of market power over consumers. Drawing on game theory, this perspective proposes an elaborate process of move and counter-move, threat and collusion, all demanding the ruthless calculation and steady nerves characteristic of the Classical tradition. Finally, the Systemic perspective points to fundamental differences between international rivals, their resources and their objectives. In particular, the Systemic critique of international business highlights the role of the nation state in the overseas expansion of Chinese, Korean and Japanese enterprise. In the terms of game theory, state-backed multinationals, playing by different rules, are likely to prove 'bad competitors' (Porter 1985).

Internationalization, in the form of FDI began to take its modern form in the late nineteenth century. The Victorian and Edwardian era saw the creation of many of the great vertically integrated multinationals that we know today – colonial plantation companies such as Lever Brothers (now Unilever) investing in West African vegetable oil plantations, Cadbury's in cocoa and Dunlop in rubber. Britain, the great imperial power of the day, dominated world international business, accounting for 45.5 per cent of the world's total stock of FDI in 1914 (Figure 5.2). The period after the Second World War saw the next great surge of FDI, as 'Pax Americana' supplanted 'Pax Britannica'. American companies such as General Motors, IBM and ITT developed manufacturing bases around the world, constituting for a weakened post-war Europe 'the American challenge' (Servan-Schreiber 1969). By 1960 the United States accounted for 48.3 per cent of world FDI. The 1980s, however, saw the decline of American economic power and the emergence of the Japanese, by a small margin the largest foreign direct investor in the world. But the world's last super-power climbed back during the 1990s to a quarter share of foreign direct investment. Meanwhile, Japan sank back well behind the ancient imperial power, the United Kingdom.

But the great puzzle remains about FDI: why do it at all? Rather than go to all the trouble, risk and expense of setting up and managing manufacturing operations in a strange country, why not export? If transport costs are prohibitive, why not simply license or sell your technology and brands to someone who knows the territory well, and who can manage directly and adapt to local conditions? This, after all, is what Pilkington's did with its float-glass technology around the world and General Foods did with its Birds Eye frozen-food brand. Pilkington's and General Foods simply took their international profits in the steady form of royalties.

The advocates of 'internalization' answer the puzzle of FDI by treating it as just another form of diversification explicable in terms of transactions costs. Rugman (1980) argues that companies prefer to co-ordinate their international transactions by hierarchy because of the special problems of

Figure 5.2 **Shares of foreign direct investment: Japan, United Kingdom and United States** (world share, 1914–60: OECD share 1971–98)

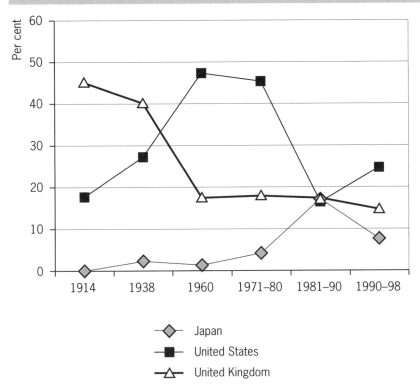

Sources: Dunning 1988; OECD International Direct Investment Statistics Yearbook.

overseas trade. Both the lack of legal control over opportunistic cheating and the distortions introduced by tariffs and customs delays make international markets much less efficient than domestic ones. Teece (1986) further points out that R&D and brand assets are particularly difficult to trade internationally, being hard to value, and so argues that knowledge-intensive industries are especially likely to set up their own operations overseas. Indeed, he finds that the extent of multinational operations by US corporations is positively correlated with the importance of advertising and R&D expenditures. IBM and Procter & Gamble are the perfect exemplars of such knowledge-intensive American multinationals.

As well as explaining the multinational patterns of particular sectors and kinds of industry, the internalization approach can help account for the secular growth of FDI relative to simple market trading relations. According to Dunning (1988), up to 1870 FDI was limited first because goods tended to be fairly simple and were easily traded in world markets and second because managerial and communications technologies were so rudimentary that the transaction costs of internalization would have been very high. However, recalling Chandler's (1977) arguments, the mass production and mass distribution companies emerging around the turn of the century simply could not afford the risk of interruptions to market

supplies and therefore made the investment in vertically integrated production of raw materials – hence the plantation and extraction companies
such as Lever Brothers and Shell. The post-war period saw the American
development of many new technologies, which US firms preferred to
transfer by direct production in overseas markets because licensing of
rapidly changing and uncodified new technologies was too difficult.
Moreover, improved organizational methods have made it increasingly
possible for multinationals to co-ordinate internally specialized units
across the world in order to maximize various local comparative advantages. Thus during the 1960s and 1970s, IBM was a pioneer in developing
specialist factories and R&D facilities throughout the world, with no less
than fifteen factories and nine laboratories in Europe alone (Ballance
1987). At the same time, tariffs or the threat of tariffs have reintroduced
international market imperfections – hence the switch of Japanese manufacturers from exports to FDI throughout the United States and Europe.
Japanese companies have also had to respond to local political pressures
to support national technological development, leading to the establishment of R&D laboratories in Taiwan by Matsushita and in Singapore by
Panasonic (Sadanori 1999).

From the internalization point of view, then, multinationals are simply
searchers after efficiency, ready to substitute markets for hierarchies as the
balance of transaction costs changes, and then passing on the benefits to
consumers. In keeping with the Darwinian presumptions of the
Evolutionary perspective from which it comes, the internalization argument does not necessarily assume a precise, risk-adjusted cost-benefit
analysis of markets against hierarchies. In practice, such an analysis would
usually be impossible. The assumption, rather, is that the competitive
forces of the market will normally winnow out those multinationals who
have not, somehow, got the balance right (Hennart 1988, 1991).

Critics from a Systemic perspective warn, of course, that there may be
something else at work other than pure market forces. Efficiency explana-
tions alone do not easily explain the direction of international vertical
integration: it has always tended to be Western manufacturing companies
that have integrated backwards, rather than developing countries' raw
materials producers integrating forwards. The Swiss, not the East Africans,
control the dominant brand for coffee. The efficiency argument does not
account either for the correlation of FDI surges with expansions in political power the golden years of British and American imperialism were also
those of greatest relative FDI. The histories of British Petroleum in the
Middle East and ITT in South America are closely linked with the foreign
policies of their respective nation-states. These companies successes seem
to owe as much to winning home government support for overturning
inconvenient regimes (in Iran or Chile) as to simple transaction cost efficiency. Finally, again, many multinationals hardly operate in the freely
competitive markets posited by the Evolutionary theorist of natural selection: companies such as IBM, Nestlé and NEC are not easily to be winnowed out by the markets they so heftily domineer.

The oligopolistic nature of multinationals opens up their strategies to
the alternative insights of Classical game theory (von Neumann and
Morgenstern 1944; Oster 1990; Graham 1991). Rather than treating the

foreign investment decision as a scrupulous process of comparing transaction costs, game theorists focus ruthlessly on competitor interactions. The international moves and countermoves of game-playing oligopolies have very little to do with maximizing efficiency, and more to do with the defence of market domination (see 'Game theory').

Game theory

Game theory extends the focus of strategic analysis to include the anticipated reaction of competitors. In the oligopolistic world of game theory, competitors are few and well known. Strategic moves are highly visible and are likely to make a substantial impact on the profits of fellow oligopolists. The various players in an industry are usually stable over time, and therefore engage in repeated interactions, Negotiation, collusion and equilibrium become possible, but aggression will provoke punitive counter-actions.

Competition in game theory, then, resembles the claimed logic for the stand-off between nuclear powers: policies of mutually assured destruction (MAD) become rational because they ensure that no-one ever launches a nuclear attack. The United States and old Soviet Union might not have liked each other, and heartily wished the other would disappear, but for nearly half a century neither side was prepared to launch any direct attack for fear of sparking-off a sequence of counter-attacks ending in the destruction of both. In just the same way, Procter & Gamble and Unilever may be in direct competition but, as old rivals in many markets, they have learned to live with each other in an uneasy peace. For them, 'MADness' would be for either of them to launch an all-out price war whose escalation would ultimately eliminate the oligopolistic profits of them both.

In these kinds of oligopolistic stand-offs, the preservation of a rough kind of peace depends on all participants knowing that any disturbance is bound to set off a mutually disastrous train of events. To preserve stability in the game, therefore, all participants must maintain both sufficient parity to punish potential transgressors and the reputation for being willing to take the risks of retaliation. Equilibrium would be jeopardized either if any participant became powerful and secure enough to launch an all-out war which it could actually win or if one of the participants looked like being soft on aggression. Again Cold War examples can illustrate. In the, 1970s, the balance of power was threatened by a loss of confidence in NATO's commitment to all-out nuclear war in retaliation against any aggression: the alliance had to restore its reputation by switching to a more credible strategy of 'flexible response' based on tactical nuclear weapons. Later, the American Strategic Defense Initiative (SDI) – a supposed umbrella against nuclear attack – threatened to be even more destabilizing. Because the SDI would remove the Soviet Union's capacity for effective retaliation, it would no longer be 'MAD' for the United States to try a nuclear confrontation.

Sources: Dixit and Nabeluff 1991;
Oster 1990

The significance of FDI decisions in game theory is that they may provide the sort of competitive advantage that would allow one player to make a successful attack on its fellow oligopolies, over-turning the existing balance of power (Knickerbocker 1973). Thus the first-mover abroad may gain market knowledge, technological advantages, economies of scale or whatever that are not available to its domestic rivals which have stayed at home. If this danger exists, the safest response for the other players in the home oligopoly is always to match each and every move abroad made by any of their rivals. By following closely, they can ensure that anything their rival has got, they have got too: no-one will gain a potentially destabilizing competitive advantage over the others.

This nervous matching activity was exactly what Knickerbocker (1973) discovered in his study of American FDI between 1948 and 1967. He found that FDI activity tended to concentrate in short time periods: 47 per cent of all FDI by his 197 US corporations in particular sectors in particular countries were clustered in three-year peaks. In other words, a move by one company into a particular country sector prompted a panic rush by its domestic rivals into the same country sector. This bunching of FDI is particularly pronounced in oligopolistic industries. Yu and Ito's (1989) comparison of US tyre manufacturers, a highly concentrated industry, with the US textile industry, relatively competitive, found the same sheep-like reactions amongst the oligopolists: rival tyre manufacturers promptly countered each other's FDI by equivalent overseas moves, while in the textile industry there was no significant bunching.

As well as explaining the overseas moves of domestic rivals, game theory can illuminate the international strategies of rivals from different countries. According to Graham (1990), FDI in different countries can be seen as an 'exchange of threats' between oligopolistic players in the same industry game. A move by a foreign multinational into home markets obviously constitutes a threat to the home players, especially if the pay-offs to aggressive strategies thereby become unequal. Thus Hamel and Pralahad (1985) consider the predicament of American domestic television producers such as RCA and Zenith when they faced Japanese entry in the 1970s. The Americans responded violently in their home market, but the price cuts and marketing spends blitzed margins in the market on which they depended for all their profits, while only affecting a small part of the invaders' total business. Because the Americans had no presence in the Japanese market, they were unable to implement aggressive counter-moves where they could actually hurt their antagonists more than they would hurt themselves.

Critical to multinational strategy, therefore, is the capacity to exchange meaningful threats (Graham 1990). A move by a foreign multinational into a local market should be matched immediately by the home multinationals: if the invader tries to spoil the home market, they can respond in kind. Exactly this sort of reciprocal reaction was captured by Flowers' (1976) study of European FDI in the United States between 1914 and 1967. Using a similar approach to Knickerbocker's (1973), he found that in highly oligopolistic industries European companies' FDI in the United States tended to concentrate in clumps immediately after surges of American investment in their own home markets. In other words, a great deal of European FDI was defensive in this period, warning the Americans not to upset home oligopolies or they would spoil theirs.

Cowling and Sugden (1987) conclude that multinational strategy is a game of creating and defending oligopolistic positions from which to extract uncompetitive profits from dominated consumers. The more multinational players are, the greater their advantage. A proliferation of country investments improves the ability to retaliate against aggressors in a gradual non-destructive way: the defender can fire warning shots in small markets first, only building up to total war in major markets if the aggressor does not back down. A wide spread of markets also makes it possible to cross-subsidize the battle in particular markets – as the Japanese television manufacturers knew, being relatively more multinational enhances a company's capacity to fight hard in one market safe from retaliation in other markets. Finally, networks of international joint ventures and alliances improve information on competitor moves, while also providing hostages against irregular action. The formation of joint ventures between rivals is like the exchange of sons between medieval kings: misbehaviour can be punished by execution. Thus the eight airline Oneworld alliance has been accused of simply being a cover for the two largest companies, American Airlines and British Airways, to protect their joint dominance of transatlantic travel (*Aviation Week and Space Technology*, 23 August 1999).

A critical assumption underlying most game theory approaches to international competition is that all participants are playing by the same basic rules. The expected outcome is some sort of collusive equilibrium, where exchange of threats ensures a rough kind of peace in which established multinationals can continue to enjoy their oligopolistic profits. Sharing Classical rationality, multinationals become, in Michael Porter's (1985) terminology, 'good competitors', offering sufficient challenge to prevent complacency while never enough to disturb the balance. Porter's (1985) advice, then, is that powerful players should preserve some gentle competition rather than fight for complete market dominance; followers should shelter under the umbrellas of industry leaders rather than attempting all-out attack. If all competitors recognize and play by the same rules, self-destructive battles over market share can be avoided (Porter 1985: 213).

The Systemic perspective, however, warns that in global competition such 'good competitors' will be hard to find. Competitors from different countries may have different resource advantages and different objectives, especially if backed by their nation states. The shock to American manufacturing in recent decades may have come in part because years of collusion had created mistaken expectations about competitors and blunted their competitive edge.

Certainly, Americans accuse the Japanese of being 'bad competitors' (Brouthers and Werner 1990). According to these authors, the Japanese are able to play by different rules because of the longterm support given to them by their banks, the selective industrial policies of the Ministry for International Trade and Industry (MITI) and the relative absence of hostile takeovers in Japan. All these factors support the typical expansionist Japanese strategy of long-term investment in market share that has been so devastating in Western markets.

The very different orientations of Japanese and Western multinationals come out in Doyle *et al.*'s (1992) comparison of the strategies of ninety matched Japanese, American and British companies competing in the UK market. Doyle and his colleagues found that four out of five of the Japanese managers gave aggressive growth or market domination as their strategic objective, against only half of the American managers and one-fifth of the British managers. Only a quarter of the Japanese companies described 'good short-term profits' as their objective, against four-fifths of their American and British competitors. Given these different orientations, when fighting head-to-head in the market-place, Western companies are likely to give up well before the Japanese.

What Americans call 'bad competitors' are, of course, tough competitors. With different priorities and time horizons, Japanese companies are not likely to accede to the tacit collusion common to Western oligopolies or to retreat in the face of the same attacks. Threats will be ignored and outright warfare fought to the bitter end. Thus the launch of IBM's advanced 370 series computer at the end of the 1960s was a knock-out blow to rival American manufacturers such as General Electric and RCA, who left the market. But IBM could not crush its infant Japanese competitors. MITI reorganized the six Japanese computer manufacturers into three groups, initiated the 3.5 Generation programme, and funded half the computer industry's research during the mid–1970s (Fransman 1990). Thus, while GE and RCA caved in, Hitachi, Fujitsu and NEC all survived to take leading positions in the world computer industry of the 1980s.

In short, game theory can provide vital insights into oligopolistic competition so long as all players are following the same rules. It gives a less reliable guide if competitors do not conform to Classical rationalities. In international competition in particular, entrepreneurial nation-states refuse to follow the rules of profit maximization. Thus Amsden (1989) shows how, in South Korea, light industries have steadily been more profitable, but none the less the state has channelled investment into heavy industries such as steel, chemicals and shipbuilding which could be oriented towards export markets. Korea's own computer initiative, bringing together Hyundai, Goldstar and Samsung in the 1980s, was called the 'Blue House Project' so closely was it connected to the President's official residence (Amsden 1989).

Even as the chaebol were being pressured to restructure in the wake of the Asian crisis of 1997–98, the Chinese Communist government launched its strategy to 'grasp the large, release the small'. Large state-owned companies such as consumer electronics company Changhong, domestic appliance company Haier or oil company Sinopec are now being promoted as the new chaebol, designed to launch China against international competition just as in Korea a generation earlier. A Chinese spokesman declared: 'We Chinese companies have a common interest in guarding our market. The common enemy is overseas manufacturers' (Yatsko 1998). The Chinese government promises lavish bank loans, tax breaks and R&D subsidies for its national champions. It is not likely that these emergent multinationals are likely to play by the 'rules' assumed in the Classical tradition.

In conclusion, both the Classical and Evolutionary accounts claim for internationalization major strategic advantages, but each emphasizes different aspects. Evolutionists see the internalization of international activities as a major source of gains in competitive efficiency. The Classical game theoretic approach is more cut-throat, viewing international moves as part of an elaborate game of pre-empting and countering competitors. Finally, Systemic theorists are sceptical about the pure efficiency of internationalization, suspecting more imperialistic motives. They also warn the Classicists that, in a complex diverse world, international strategy is a game of rough and tumble in which not everybody will stick to the same rules.

Conclusions

This chapter has looked at three important types of strategy – innovation, diversification and internationalization – through the different lenses of the Classical, Evolutionary, Processual and Systemic perspectives. In each case, the various perspectives have offered different insights into effective strategies in these areas. Often the advice from each perspective has been directly contradictory. Rarely has the evidence been conclusive in any direction. But the controversy should be enough at least to help strategic decision-makers escape the glib strategic nostrums of the pundits and to think hard about the alternatives.

In innovation, the dominant Classical model of market-oriented R&D has been challenged from nearly every direction. Schumpeterians have pointed to how innovation can be used to dominate markets, while Marxians have stressed the value of technological innovation in securing internal control. Processualists have warned against the over-management of innovation and highlighted the entrenched conservatism of industries in practice. There is little evidence that high investment in innovation pays anyway. Finally, Systemic theorists have doubted the universality of the market-oriented model and have cynically suggested that its popularity with marketeers may have something to do with their own professional self-interest. The conclusion must be that, in innovation strategy, market orientation is not the be all and end all.

There is no unanimity about diversification and takeovers either. Classicists and Evolutionists alike urge diversification as a means of managing resources and transactions to optimal advantage. They conclude that diversification must pay, or there would not be so many diversified corporations around. Systemic theorists are more sceptical. They notice that diversified corporations have not been around for that long anyway, and that many economies do not have the same patterns of diversification as the United States. From the Systemic perspective, diversification is suspected as reflecting more the managerial interest in growth than the shareholder interest in maximum profits. The implication for the strategist is that, before undertaking any diversification, it would be well to stop and question the motives: will the new activities really benefit shareholders?

Lastly, the split over internationalization has been between Evolutionary theorists of internalization, the Classical proponents of game theory and the Systemic emphasis on political intervention. For the Evolutionists, internationalization reflects the same logic as diversification, the integration of activities in order to maximize efficiency. In this account, international strategy reduces to maintaining cost advantage. For the game theorists, internal efficiency does not matter so much as the constant battle of wits against oligopolistic competitors. The moves and counter-moves of internationalization are about making sure that no-one achieves a decisive competitive advantage that is threatening to established oligopolies. Sometimes efficiency should be sacrificed to maintain the capacity and credibility of retaliation. But the Systemic theorists warn that these elaborate oligopolistic games may be futile against international competitors with different motives, time horizons and resources. In international competitive strategy, it can be a fatal mistake to assume that everybody is fighting on a level playing field. Strategists should seek, from the state or elsewhere, some unfair advantages of their own.

6 Managing strategy

*General Motors has no mind that can be said to be
unwaveringly focused on profit. It has no mind in
which complete data resides and in which the
necessary calculations are made. In fact, it has no
mind at all.*

(Bartlett 1989: 103)

Introduction

The problem for strategy is that organizations are, literally, 'mindless'.
They have no unity and collectively they are rather stupid. Yet the notion
of 'strategy' implies that all the multitudinous individuals who make up
an organization can be united around the effective pursuit of a coherent
goal. This was the challenge that Alfred Sloan (1963) wrestled with on a
grand scale at General Motors. For him, the solution lay in imposing hierarchical structures that tapered to the singular intelligence of himself. He
was to be the 'mind' of General Motors.

This chapter addresses strategy implementation – organizing strategy
and getting strategy to change. On the organization of strategy, the innovations of Alfred Sloan have won the support of both Classical and
Evolutionary theorists. Efficient co-ordination requires that diversification
strategies should be matched by divisional organizational structures. For
Classicists and Evolutionists, it is obvious that structure should follow
strategy. But Processual and Systemic critics do not leave matters there.
The Processual critique points to not only how organizational structures
in practice fail to fit strategies, but how strategies can actually be shaped
by them. The direction of causality is reversed. Systemic theorists suspect
that organizational efficiency is often defined in terms of what suits the
interests of top management, and point anyway to how what is efficient
varies widely according to societal context.

The evidence that organizational structures do not always fit neatly
with business strategies reinforces the Processual argument about strategic
change. Recalling Pettigrew's (1990) point from Chapter 4, the focus of
the Classical school is on strategic choice, rather than strategic change. For

the Processualists, it is change, not choice, that is the difficult bit (Whipp *et al.* 1989). Following Cyert and March (1963), organizations are coalitions of cognitively biased, routine-loving, politically motivated and boundedly rational individuals. Getting these kinds of organizations to change takes a lot of patient coaxing and political compromise. Evolutionists take a more robust view: the best way of getting change is to make the painful costs of failure abundantly clear. Fear of takeover, dismissal or bankruptcy should be all the incentive organizations need to change rapidly and efficiently.

Strategy and structure

Top managers spend more time and energy on implementing strategies than choosing them. Strategies that are well chosen will fail because of poor implementation. Getting the organizational structures right for a particular strategy is thus clearly critical to practical success.

It is not surprising, then, that the matching of strategy to structure is also an area of fierce theoretical debate. Here, as over diversification, the Darwinian imperatives of the Evolutionary approach join with the rational logic of the Classical School. Again, Systemic theorists challenge the reality of market imperatives and the universality of the logics, while Processualists emphasize the complex and ambiguous role of organizational structure in practice.

Alfred Chandler's (1962) maxim 'structure follows strategy' dominates the field. The logic of his argument is a crucial one, theoretically and prescriptively. He presents the fit of structure to strategy as a normative injunction, but describes it in practice as a necessary adjustment to market pressures. He takes as his exemplars the large American corporations of the first half of this century – such as Du Pont, General Motors, Standard Oil (now Exxon) and Sears Roebuck – and describes how their early attempts at diversification kept ending up in organizational chaos. The problem for these early diversifiers was not strategy, but organization structure. Within their existing structures, the 'co-ordination costs' of managing widely different businesses grossly exceeded the benefits of diversification. Only when they moved from the centralized functional structures that they had developed as single businesses towards multidivisional structures for their new businesses were these companies able to make diversification strategies pay (see 'Diversification and multidivisionalization'). Companies which did not adopt new multidivisional structures in response to diversification tended to fail, as Du Pont itself nearly did, or get taken over by more structurally able companies, as for instance United States Rubber was finally taken over by Du Pont. In short, structure *has* to follow strategy.

For Oliver Williamson (1985, 1988), the success of the multidivisional structure lies in its capacity to cope with the 'bounded rationality' and 'opportunism' that undermine control in large complex organizations. The functional organization fails when the size and diversity of business produces an operational complexity beyond the capacity of top managers to comprehend, at the same time as creating scope for opportunistic pursuit of departmental rather than aggregate goals. The move to the

Diversification and multidivisionalization

According to Chandler (1962), the multidivisional structure was discovered by Du Pont as it coped with the chaos following its diversification from its original core gun-powder business. During the First World War the company had integrated backwards into the chemical raw materials necessary to sustain its vastly increased explosives production. At the same time, Du Pont began to diversify into dyestuffs, for which war had created critical shortages, and also into new civil markets, such as celluloid, paints and artificial leather, in anticipation of the peace.

What Du Pont did not do was change its old centralized functional structure, headed by an Executive Committee made up of departmental chiefs. All production remained under a single production department; all sales, under a single sales department (Figure 6.1).

The strains on the old structure became evident in the post-war recession, but structural change was resisted. Top managers saw the problem in terms of a few ill-judged diversifications and the solution in terms of divestments and tightening up existing information systems. Executive Committee members also valued their direct control over departments, each regarding the performance of their own department as their own business, not to be intruded on by colleagues. Accordingly, Irenée Du Pont, the company President, turned down the first proposals for a multidivisional structure in 1920.

By the next year, Du Pont was making serious losses, with the only profits coming from its original core explosives businesses. The sales department, used to selling bulk commodities, could not understand its new consumer businesses; responsibility for escalating stock levels was batted around between the separate manufacturing, purchasing and sales departments. Only in 1921, when the survival of the whole company was at stake, did the Executive Committee accept the multidivisional structure depicted in Figure 6.2 (overleaf). Du Pont kept to this basic multidivisional structure for the next forty years. Chandler (1962: 112) concludes: 'At Du Pont, then, structure followed strategy.'

Figure 6.1 **Du Pont structure, 1919–21**

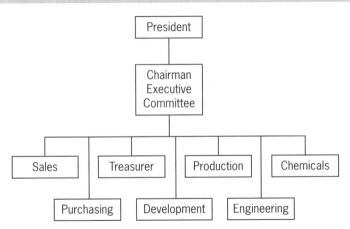

Figure 6.2 **Du Pont structure, August 1921**

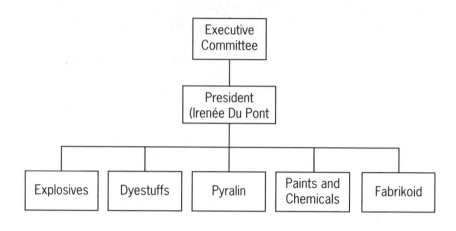

Source: Adapted from Chandler 1962

multidivisional form reduces the transaction costs of hierarchy by decentralizing operational responsibilities to smaller discrete units and making divisional managers clearly accountable for business unit performance. With information now sifted through divisional managers, and freed from departmental interests, top management can concentrate on overall strategy. The multidivisional form is the most efficient way, then, of dealing with the complexity of diversification.

Since Du Pont's first development, the spread of the multidivisional form has come partly through imitation and partly through Darwinian processes of competition. The great evolutionary advantage of the multidivisional firm is its ability to take over and absorb less well adapted competitors (Williamson 1988). The multidivisional form is the perfect structure for conglomerate strategies. Carnivores of the corporate jungle, such conglomerates gobble up weaker firms by acquisition, and digest them simply by putting new businesses alongside their existing divisions. The dominance of today's business world by the multidivisional form is due in part to its voracious appetite and excellent digestion.

As European companies diversified as well, so too did the multidivisional structure spread through Europe. By the early 1990s, 90 per cent of large British industrial corporations had divisionalized, and more than two-thirds of French and German (Mayer and Whittington 1999). However, not all is smooth. The adoption of divisional structures often lags diversification. In his historical analysis of divisionalization in the United States, Donaldson (1987: 16) found widespread failures to match strategy and structure in the approved way: '33 of the 43 corporations which were mismatched in 1959 had been in this state in 1949. This may have arisen from diversifications in the 1940s or earlier.' In other words, American businesses endured structural lags of over ten years. Perhaps the logic of multidivisionalization may not be so attractive, and the pressure of natural selection so irresistible, as Evolutionary and Classical theorists think.

Processual authors would not be surprised at such lags between strategic and structural change. Organizational processes of adjustment are always slow and imperfect. But the Processual critique goes further, attacking the very logic of strategy first, structure second. This sequence is too typical of the detached linear approach of Classical strategy. Mintzberg (1990) insists that strategies can rarely be decided in isolation from existing structures. Structures are not the infinitely plastic supports of the Classical strategist's imagination. In practice, organizational structures both enable and constrain particular strategies.

Indeed, D.J. Hall and Saias (1980) even invert Chandler's dictum to assert that 'strategy follows structure! ' Adoption of the multidivisional structure biases firms towards conglomerate strategies because they deny top managements sufficient access to the actual businesses to allow them even to see opportunities for organic expansion. For the detached top managers of multidivisional firms, the easiest option is just to buy another division to put alongside the others. Mintzberg (1990: 183), however, finally takes a more balanced view, rejecting any unilateral determination from either direction. He concludes that the relationship between strategy and structure is inextricably reciprocal: 'structure follows strategy . . . as the left foot follows the right'.

The Processual view, then, challenges the notion of organizational structures as simple tools for the efficient implementation of strategy. What tools you have determine what strategic job you undertake. But the puzzle raised by Donaldson's (1987) structural lags remains: how is it that firms are able to get away with such long delays in adjusting structures to strategies? If the Evolutionists are right, surely these laggards should have been selected out by the markets. Systemic critics of the Evolutionary perspective seize on these anomalies to challenge both the 'efficiency' of multidivisional structures and the strength of the competitive imperatives that drive them.

The companies that Chandler (1977) and Williamson (1985) discuss are the corporate giants of American business. As alleged in the previous chapter, the motives for their growth, and the profits that sustained them, were not always those simply of efficiency. As giant corporations, far from being insecure competitors, they were able to dominate their markets, and extract oligopolistic profits. For them, competitive pressures towards efficient forms of organization were easy to ignore. The case of US Steel, one of Chandler's (1977) own examplars, illustrates. Put together in 1901 by J.P. Morgan, this highly diversified leviathan resisted multidivisional organization until the 1930s. As controller of 60 per cent of the US structural steel and wire markets, half the country's pig iron and rail milling capacity and pretty much all of barbed wire production, US Steel could ignore internal efficiency and instead rely simply on exploiting its market dominance (Du Boff and Herman 1980). Until the arrival of Japanese steel in the 1970s, and the high-tech minimills of the 1980s, there were simply no competitors in the marketplace that could put US Steel under serious pressure to conform.

Thus the Evolutionary account may be part of the story, but its normative implications – structure should follow strategy – do not always seem to be as pressing as its advocates assert. For large corporations – such as Du Pont or US Steel – the pressure of natural selection provides insufficient incentive to change. They can get away with allowing structure to follow strategy with a very considerable lag. This lag may entail a performance penalty, but then, as the Systemic perspective warns again, large corporations are not always run simply for shareholders' profit. Indeed, it may be that the multidivisional structure is at least as well fitted to protecting top management's interests as to maximizing the returns to shareholders.

For top management, Bauer and Cohen (1983) allege, the advantage of the multidivisional form is its capacity to disempower both owners and middle managers. With regard to ownership interests, the large diversified multidivisional firm is both too complex for outside shareholders readily to understand and too big and unwieldy for easy takeover in the case of underperformance. As for internal politics, the relegation of functional managers to the details of business unit operations, and their separation from strategy-making for the firm as a whole, creates a barrier between middle managers and main-board decision-makers that is hard to cross. Functional specialists, excluded from a general knowledge of the firm as a complete entity, are unable to challenge the logics of top-level corporate strategy. In these ways, then, the multidivisional firm's strategic direction becomes too complex for shareholders to supervise and too remote for middle managers to question. The multidivisional form thus serves not just efficiency, but the security of incumbent top managerial cliques (cf. Francis 1983).

The managerial group most favoured by the multidivisional form are, according to Fligstein (1990), the financial and accounting professionals. He argues that the rise to the top in American business of managers with finance backgrounds since the 1950s (see Chapter 3) has created a new regime of 'finance control', superseding the previous regime of 'sales and marketing control' established in the 1920s. The strategies associated with finance control are not necessarily profit-maximizing, but rather those which financiers have managed to promote as the accepted way of doing business in American culture. Finance professionals have promoted multi-divisionalization because this form of organization demands their skills of detached financial comparison and monitoring. Multidivisionalization became accepted as the American way of doing business because it corresponded with the institutional expectations of rapid growth and short-term financial performance made prominent in the last three decades. Market analysts, consultants, business school academics and their alumni came to regard this organizational form as the mark of the modern business, and doubted the competence of those top managers who clung to older functional forms. Rather than risk their scorn, once the diversified multidivisional firm had become the norm, it became sociologically efficient to conform with business fashion, even at the expense of economic efficiency.

This Systemic stress on the historical contingency of multidivisionalization is paralleled by a similar concern for the cultural specificity of forms of organization. We have seen already how the American logic of product diversification does not apply universally, especially in developing countries (see Chapter 5); in the same way, American forms of organization do not necessarily translate overseas.

Keiretsu – old and new

On the face of it, Japan's *keiretsu* are similar multi-unit enterprises to the diversified, divisionalized corporations of the United States. But that is just the surface.

To start with, the origins of the multi-unit enterprise in Japan upset Chandler's (1962) chronology. The diversified family controlled *zaibatsu* originated in the seventeenth century and began to devolve responsibility into semi-autonomous subsidiaries during the late nineteenth-century industrialization of the Meiji period (Yamazaki 1988). The aim was not efficient co-ordination, but to allow the infusion of outside capital into new businesses at the same time as retaining family control through 51 per cent ownership of subsidiaries. In 1908, Mitsubishi organized its mining, banking and ship-building subsidiaries as independent profit centres, with managerial and investment autonomy roughly equivalent to that developed by Du Pont and General Motors a decade and a half later (McMillan 1985). The diversified *zaibatsu* groups were broken up by the Americans during the post-war occupation but soon re-emerged after independence in 1952. The Mitsubishi group was re-established in 1954, the Mitsui group in 1959 (Yamazaki 1988).

The post-war groups have generally taken the looser form of *keiretsu*. The new *keiretsu* groupings work partly through interlocking minority shareholdings, partly through reliance on group banks for financial support and partly through mutual shareholding (Anchordoguy 1990). For example, the Sumitomo bank is at the centre of a *keiretsu* in which it has traditionally held large stakes in both NEC, the world's largest chip manufacturer, and electronics company Matsushita. Sumitomo group members tend overwhelmingly to buy NEC computers. But also important are the informal links between *keiretsu* group members. Group presidents typically meet regularly in 'Friday clubs' where conflicts of interest and matters of mutual advantage are discussed and resolved in a simple spirit of co-operation and sense of long-term relationship. There is much less need for formal hierarchy and legal precision than in the American system.

At the beginning of the twenty-first century, some of the old *keiretsu* are restructuring, but others are emerging. Since 1981, Masayoshi Son has constructed a new Japanese *keiretsu* in the form of Softbank Corporation. With substantial stakes in 300 Internet companies such as Yahoo!, E*Trade and Buy-com, Softbank has become a 'cyber-*keiretsu*' worth $200 billion in February 2000. Softbank officially describes its group of companies as a 'family', and there is considerable inter-trading and assistance. The company attributes its success to Son's 'innovative management style. He delegates most of the decisions to each unit's CEO and operates the company as a client/server organization, rather than a hierarchic pyramidal organization' (www.softbank.com).

Figure 6.3 **Softbank: cyber-*keiretsu*?**

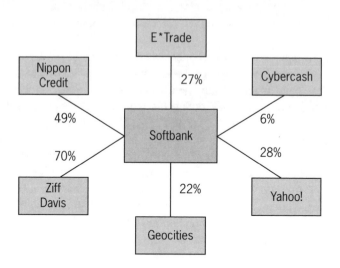

Source: www.softbank.com

Contrasting the Far East with the United States, Hamilton and Biggart (1988) emphasize the role of culture and history in explaining the emergence of prevailing organizational forms (see '*Keiretsu* – old and new'). The diversified business groups of Japan and the *chaebol* of Korea might look from the outside much like Western corporations, and generally compete with them effectively, but their structures were not designed simply to minimize the transaction costs following expansion and diversification. The Japanese business groups originated long before Japanese industrialization, stemming from the *zaibatsu* merchant houses such as Mitsui that flourished during the Tokugawa era (1603–1867) (Hamilton and Biggart 1988). Korea's *chaebol* grew from the *zaibatsu*-type structures imposed by the Japanese during the pre-Second World War period of colonial occupation. Taiwan, by contrast, has managed to achieve economic success even though it has clung to the traditional structures of Chinese family business and resisted the creation of large-scale multidivisional organizations (Whitley 1990). There, diversification is managed typically by tenuously linked strings of relatives. Throughout the Chinese world, *guanxi* networks of informal relationships form the strong ties through which business can be done without the formal structures of an integrated firm (Tsang 1998).

Indeed, Asia's ancient *keiretsu* and *guanxi* networks are now proposed as the model for advanced capitalism around the world (Castells 1996). Networks between firms make redundant the old model of vertically integrated companies like Ford in the past, where the same organization controlled everything right back to the rubber plantations that supplied the tyres. Companies like Toyota are able to manage extended networks of suppliers that are far more flexible and better at creating and sharing knowledge (Dyer and Nobeoka 2000). Likewise, networks within firms can exchange knowledge more effectively than the typical 'chimneys' of the multidivisional firm (Pettigrew and Fenton 2000; Whittington *et al.* 1999). Divisions communicate formally by going up the hierarchy, across and then finally down, not directly between themselves. As Ghoshal and Bartlett (1995) observe, 'divisions divide'. According to Volberda (1998), the loose fluidity of networks, internally and externally, are much more suited to this 'postmodern world' than the rigid hierarchies of the traditional multidivisional (see 'Postmodern strategy?').

Postmodern strategy?

Classical strategy was developed by such pioneers as Ansoff (1965) and Chandler (1962) in the hey-day of 'modernism', the 1950s and the 1960s. Modernism as a philosophy puts its place in rational analysis, universal solutions and remote control. The stark architecture of Mies van der Rohe and Le Corbusier expressed the modernist philosophy more generally: monotonous, perfectly symmetrical tower-blocks, imposed on cities around the world regardless of context, simple 'machines for living'.

From the 1970s onwards, postmodernism has become the fashion. Postmodernism is sceptical of formal rationality, values local contexts and treats us as individuals, capable of construing the world for ourselves and even of taking a joke. Buildings are now quirky and colourful, friendlier to their surroundings and to their inhabitants. Business too is becoming more 'postmodern'. All Chandler's (1962) original presuppositions are challenged by the Processualists. The rigid separation of strategy from operations is no longer valid in a knowledge-based age. The claim that managers can control through rational and detached analysis a wide range of businesses is scorned by those who emphasize the contextual skills of particular industries. The tall hierarchies and strict divisions of the multidivisional are now replaced by flat organizations and 'boundaryless' networks.

See Appignanesi and Garratt 1995; Starkey and Whittington 1999;
Lowendahl and Revang 1998; Whittington and Mayer 2001.

In short, what Williamson and Chandler take to be the universal model of contemporary enterprise – underpinned by the economics of transaction costs and driven by the competitive forces of the market – in fact turns out to be an ethnocentric and historicist ideal. Culture and history may determine organizational forms as much as the abstract logics of efficiency and markets. The crude transfer of contemporary Anglo-Saxon organizational models to other cultural contexts invites failure at worst, reinterpretation at best.

To summarize, the Classical and Evolutionary advice that structure must follow strategy may be basically sound, but it is also a bit simplistic. Where firms enjoy oligopolistic security, or are subject to managerial control, or operate in different societies, Systemic theorists point out that the link between strategy and structure may not follow the precise forms of the textbooks. Sometimes it will be futile or even dangerous to impose Classical multidivisional structures upon diversified businesses. Again the Systemic advice is to be sensitive to context. The Processual message, moreover, is not to expect that the relationship between strategy and structure necessarily follows the neat sequential logic of Classical theory. Organizational structures do not change that easily.

Strategic change

From the last section, we saw how slow and difficult structural change can be in practice: Irenée Du Pont resisted abandoning the functional structure until the point of crisis (Chandler 1962); Donaldson's (1987) sample of large American firms seemed to delay matching their structure to new strategies for decades at a time. The Processual stress on the complex conservative nature of organizations gains still more force over the issue of overall strategic change. For some Processualists, the generic capacity to handle strategic change is now the critical source of competitive advantage (Pettigrew and Whipp 1991). In today's fast moving environment, more specific sources of advantage, rooted in particular technologies or markets for instance, are liable quickly to be superseded. Truly sustainable advantage comes from the internal ability to adapt and learn.

But history is littered with managers apparently unable to adapt to new and threatening circumstances, and suffering the penalty of dismissal. Studies of corporate 'turnarounds' following periods of organizational decline repeatedly confirm the necessity of hiring new chairmen or chief executives in order to achieve strategic change and recovery. New top managers were required in 73 per cent of Bibeault's (1982) successful turnarounds, by 87 per cent of Slatter's (1984) and by 65 per cent of Grinyer *et al.*'s (1988). Often, managers recruited from outside the organization altogether are necessary to achieve the changes required for turnaround: in Bibeault's (1982) study, 61 per cent of the new top managers were outsiders. Insiders seem reluctant to impose the radical changes often necessary for recovery. Likewise, Whittington's (1991b) examination of strategic responses to the recession in the early 1980s found that harsh strategies of rationalization and refocusing tended to be adopted only after attempts at more moderate strategies, and then were imposed by new outsider chief executives.

This reliance on outsiders provides us with rather a gloomy perspective on the capacity of incumbent managers to achieve substantial change. From an Evolutionary perspective, this managerial incapacity is neither surprising nor very significant. In Hannan and Freeman's (1988) population ecology account, the failure of individual firms and managers does not matter; what is important is a plentiful supply of new firms and managers to replenish the population as it is winnowed out by the Darwinian selection processes of the market. As the rate of environmental change accelerates, one should not expect adaptation by existing enterprises. The process of achieving optimal fit to established ecological niches naturally leaves incumbent firms and managers with little slack to adapt to subsequent changes. Adaptation comes at the population level, as redundant old organizations disappear and new better adapted actors emerge to replace them.

To the individual capitalist or manager facing environmental change, this contempt for the fate of existing enterprises may appear too coldly detached. It does raise a salutary question, however. Organizational survival is not necessarily the highest objective. The best approach to change may not always be by internal adaptation; it may be by breaking up and abandoning existing structures altogether. Adaptation comes through releasing the human and capital resources tied up in old structures back onto the market, to be reconstituted in entirely new combinations. To look for change internally, within established parameters, may be maladaptive and, finally, fruitless.

However, not all Evolutionary accounts are so bleak. The agency perspective believes that the threat of market failure is generally enough to motivate change, even if sometimes at the last moment. Like the managerial economists, agency theorists see resistance to change coming from the conflicting interests between firms' principals (their owners) and the agents (the managers) they employ to run them (Jensen and Meckling 1976; Eisenhardt 1989). When times are hard or new directions needed, top managers may resist belt-tightening, the firing of buddies and the abandoning of cherished businesses or exciting new ventures (Kimberley and Zajac 1988). None the less, the agency theorists maintain that principals can successfully coerce change by the clever manipulation of market pressures (see 'The CalPERS effect').

The CalPERS effect

CalPERS – short for the California Public Employees' Retirement System – is America's largest pension fund. It is also a determined campaigner for investor rights, using its massive shareholding power against lackadaisical or self-serving top management teams. Its annual focus list of ten or so poor performing or badly governed corporations is respected by the good, feared by the bad. Amongst companies to have been targeted are such major names as Advanced Micro Devices, Apple Computer, Crown Cork & Seal, Heinz Foods, ITT and National Semiconductor.

CalPERS gets results, according to a study of sixty-two companies targeted by the fund. On average, these companies trailed the Standard & Poor's 500 Index by 89 per cent in the five year period before CalPERS acted. In the five year period following CalPERS action, these same companies outperformed the Index by an average of 23 per cent.

Source: www.calpers-governance.org; Smith 1996.

For agency theorists, the solution to the problem of untrustworthy agents lies in increasing exposure to the pressures of both the market for corporate control and the managerial labour market (Fama 1980; Stiglitz 1985). The threat of takeover for underperformance, with the fear of wholesale dismissals of existing upper echelons, should be enough to keep managers disciplined. Adaptive profit-maximizing management can be secured in these terms by ensuring open financial information and preventing poison-pills, shark-repellants, golden parachutes and other devices for protecting against takeovers. Reputation for good performance is likely also to be valued by senior managers wanting to maximize their value in the labour market. Again policies to encourage open information are important to improving the workings of the managerial labour market, but so too is giving access to searching business journalists and management academics. Shareholders need to promote an informed, flexible managerial labour market in which good performers are head-hunted, weak ones face unemployment.

Many companies apply the agency approach to change internally. Under the financial control model identified by Goold and Campbell (1987), conglomerates manage their subsidiaries not only by exploiting the information and reporting advantages of ownership, but also by importing the pressures of the external markets for control and managerial labour. Head offices exert discipline over potentially recalcitrant subsidiary managers by declaring their readiness to fire poorly performing managers and to divest loss-making subsidiaries. Goold and Campbell (1987) report that, within one BTR group, four out of sixteen subsidiary managing directors had been fired within three years. At Hanson Trust, the archetypal conglomerate of the last decade, one director declared: 'All of our businesses are for sale all of the time' (Campbell *et al.* 1990: 28). The message to managers was that Hanson would sell their companies to anyone who thought they could make more money out of them, and who would pay for the privilege of trying. Under Lord Hanson, managers change – or else! (See 'Putting the e into GE')

This agency approach to dealing with managerial conservatism or self-interest relies on the big stick of market pressure. Although it accepts the Systemic account of managerial motives, and shares the Classical belief that, by hook or by crook, managers can be made into rational profit-

---

Putting the e into GE

General Electric, *Fortune* magazine's most admired corporation in both 1998 and 1999, was slow to recognize the Internet. As GE's legendary chairman and chief executive, Jack Welch, admitted at his shareholders' annual meeting in 2000, the company's slow response was a classic case of 'cognitive bias': 'We thought the creation and operation of web sites was mysterious, Nobel Prize stuff, the province of the wild-eyed and purple-haired'.

Welch launched a ruthless e-business catch-up programme based on internal Darwinism. The programme's title was 'destroyyourbusiness.com'. GE managers were turned into entrepreneurial cannibals – destroying their old businesses in order to create the new. Welch had no pangs for laggards in his portfolio: 'The attic is getting full again. This way we'll get an Internet focus and clear out some crap.' His only fear was whether the Darwinian struggle would be fierce enough: 'Do we have the right gene pool? Do people who join big companies want to break glass?'

Sources: *Financial Times*, 9 November 1999, 27 April 2000;
Fortune, 27 September 1999.

maximizers, its argument is ultimately Evolutionary: profitability is secured by the rough justice of the markets. The very fact that not all managers do succeed in changing at least sends out a valuable message. The takeover of a prominent corporation, or the dismissal of a well-known business personality, serves to promote change elsewhere. As Voltaire was told on the execution of the hapless Admiral Blake, it may not be fair, but at least it encourages the others.

Table 6.1 **The 1999 Fortune Global 500: (The world's largest firms by total revenues)**

Rank		$bn	Founded
1	General Motors	161	1908
2	DaimlerChrysler	155	1883/1890
3	Ford Motor	144	1903
4	Wal-Mart	139	1962
5	Mitsui	109	1673
6	Itochu	109	1858
7	Mitsubishi	107	1870
8	Exxon	101	1882
9	General Electric	100	1892
10	Toyota	100	1926
11	Royal Dutch/Shell	94	1870
12	Murubeni	94	1858

Source: www.fortune.com/fortune/global 500; Derdack 1988.

Processual theorists take a softer line on strategic change. To start with, there can be basic credibility problems in bludgeoning large organizations with threats to survival. As Table 6.1 indicates, the average age of the world's twelve largest corporations by turnover in 1999 – the onset of the internet era – was 126 years old. Only one of these companies – Wal-Mart – even had its origins in the second half of the twentieth century. Many of these companies, moreover, had only made incremental changes to their basic strategies over the long years of their existence. The three largest companies in the world – General Motors, Daimler and Ford – are all still making cars just as they had around a century before. Exxon and Shell have stayed basically in oil. Rather than terrorising managers in the manner of the agency theorists, Processualists tend to prefer more gentle processes of coaxing and coaching. Some Processual writers even believe that a certain inhibition with regard to change can be a good thing.

According to the Processualists, the problem of change is first of all getting people to recognize the need for change. We saw in Chapter 4 how subjective managerial interpretations of the environment could be, especially in analysing strengths, weaknesses, opportunities and threats. Following the Carnegie School, these subjective interpretations are the inescapable result of human bounded rationality and cognitive bias.

However, most dangerously, subjectivity can become institutionalized within particular firms or industries into self-reinforcing 'recipes' (Spender 1989) or 'paradigms' (Johnson 1987) for seeing and understanding the world. Managers are selected and promoted according to how they conform with the world-views of existing top management; firms look to how their established rivals compete, and follow their example. These processes of comparison and conformity can create ways of understanding the world that become nearly impervious to discrepant information. Porac *et al.* (1989) give the example of the luxury knitwear industry of Scotland, centred on the small town of Hawick, in which all the managers from every company knew each other well. Indeed, the Hawick industry formed such a close 'cognitive community' that it could not recognize the threat represented by new colourful and stylish Italian producers – the Scottish knitwear companies would not even accept that the Italians could be counted as part of their own tightly bound industry.

The Processual solution to cognitive bias and bounded rationality is corporate 'learning' (Jones and Hendry 1992). De Geus (1988: 71), head of planning at Royal Dutch Shell, asserts that in a fast changing world 'the ability to learn faster than your competitors may be the only sustainable competitive advantage'. At Shell, therefore, corporate planning is primarily about flexibility, the changing of minds, rather than rigidity, the making of plans.

Because existing recipes or paradigms can become so fixed, change is also a matter of deliberate 'unlearning' (Nystrom and Starbuck 1984). Existing cognitive structures need to be constantly challenged by the fostering of dissent, toleration for failed experiments and acceptance of the dualistic Chinese definition of crisis, as moments of opportunity as well as danger. The collective self-reinforcing nature of existing recipes requires that both learning and unlearning processes should extend deep into the organization. Strategic learning is not just a matter for top management. Indeed, this approach to organizational learning prompts Senge (1990) to reject the Classical view of the leader as a somehow special and separate kind of individual. According to Senge, heroic individualism is a thing of the past: the 'leader's new work' is the much more modest task of creating the conditions in which everybody can learn, because everyone must adapt.

Senge's (1990) vision of the top manager as coach rather than dictator is one subscribed to by Goold and Campbell's (1987) 'strategic control' companies. In these companies, the role of the centre is first of all the fostering of open minds amongst subsidiary managers. At Vickers, the chief executive has 'a responsibility for helping managers to get their heads up over the parapet and to think more broadly from time to time'. Sir Christopher Hogg at Courtaulds claims: 'Our role at the centre is to enforce quality standards in strategic thinking and we have a role in helping to educate and develop managers' (Goold and Campbell 1987: 85–7).

Treating the problem of change as one of organizational learning is an important and attractive insight. Managers are liberated from routines; subordinates are empowered to challenge reigning orthodoxies. But the notion of organizational learning is finally a reductive and idealistic metaphor. It too easily trivializes organizational change to the level of opening up people's minds, and reduces organizational resistance to mere 'wrong-headedness' (e.g. Argyris 1991). More sophisticated Processual analyses recognize the entrenched political interests that also sustain existing organizational recipes and routines.

In the accounts of Pettigrew (1985) and Johnson (1987), strategic change is a matter of delicate political manoeuvring as well as the changing of people's minds. At ICI during the 1970s and early 1980s, the promotion of strategic change and the upwards career of John Harvey-Jones were closely connected (Pettigrew 1985). Early on Harvey-Jones used organization development consultants to stimulate new thinking: later he dropped them as his advance to the deputy chairmanship, one step from the very top, made a less overtly 'left-wing' stance appropriate. In other words, the balance of his strategy shifted from cognitive to political. At Apple, on the other hand, both powerful political interests and a stubborn refusal to learn kept the company locked into a near fatal reluctance to license properly its operating system for a decade and a half (see 'Apple bites the bullet – almost'). Licensing threatened the interests of manufacturing; it also challenged founder Steve Jobs's vision of Apple as the only company worthy to carry out his mission for the world. Even the defeat of manufacturing with the merger of hardware into software was not enough. The company blindly pursued its vision for the Mac towards effective oblivion. Strategic change required both cognitive and political change.

Apple bites the bullet – almost

Apple's Macintosh computers fulfilled the company's dream: in the phrase of the company's passionate founder, Steve Jobs, to make 'insanely great computers'. But preventing anybody else making them nearly destroyed the company.

Launched in 1984, the Mac was both an elegant piece of computer hardware and a spectacular advance in software – a Graphical User Interface four years before Microsoft's primitive Windows package. The problem was that Apple also was both a hardware manufacturer and a software house, and for more than a decade it was hardware that dominated.

As early as 1985, Microsoft was pleading with Apple to open up the software architecture of the Mac to allow clone manufacturers to produce cheaper versions and encourage the development of additional supporting software. Even though Microsoft was in bed with IBM, it warned that Apple on its own would never get enough volume to challenge the IBM PC standard and that there would not be room in the market for two types of incompatible system. But Apple had invested in state-of-the-art manufacturing facilities and was getting 95 per cent of its revenue from the sale of own-produced Macs. Clones would undercut Apple's prices and leave manufacturing exposed. The hardware operation controlled the licensing of production, and set the license fees deliberately high. The pioneering software was being used to sell nice-looking computer boxes.

During 1994, Apple's market share collapsed from 16 per cent to just 10 per cent. There was a fierce political struggle within the corporation. In April 1995, Apple reorganized, the hardware operation being merged into the software operation. The former hardware vice-president, Ian Diery, resigned. The company finally announced a more open licensing strategy and several companies, including IBM and Motorola, acquired licences to use the Mac software as

> the basis for their own manufactured computers. Clones were supposed to put the Mac market share up to 20 per cent overall.
>
> Unfortunately for this strategy at least, in 1997 Steve Jobs returned to power at the company, after an absence of twelve years. Making insanely great computers was Apple's vocation, not anybody else's. The new licensing strategy was reversed. By 1999, the Mac's share of the personal computer market was 4 per cent.
>
> Sources: Linzmayer 1999; *Macworld*, August 1995.

The danger of the purely 'learning' approach to change, therefore, is that it can lead one to underestimate one's opponents. Sympathetic coaching may not be enough. Sometimes managers may actually recognize the need for change, yet still refuse to 'learn' because they understand perfectly well the implications for their power and status. Resistance to change may not be 'stupid', as the cognitive perspective implies, but based on a very shrewd appreciation of the personal consequences.

A Processual combination of the cognitive and political perspectives warns that strategic change is likely often to be a gradual process. Pettigrew concluded from his study of the drawn-out and complex transformation of ICI between the 1960s and early 1980s:

> *This kind of process management also necessitated patience and perseverence; waiting for people to retire to exploit any policy vacuum so created; introducing known sympathisers as replacements for known sceptics or opponents; using succession occasions to combine portfolios and responsibilities and integrate thought and action in an otherwise previously factious and deadlocked area of change; backing off and waiting, or moving the pressure point for change into another area when continuing downright opposition might have endangered the success of the whole change exercise.*

(1985: 458)

Admittedly, Pettigrew's (1985) experience here is of a large bureaucratic organization, with sufficient market power never to fear complete collapse, but his picture of strategic change remains a compelling one: change emerges as an undramatic, unglamorous process of continuous manoeuvre, its longeurs punctuated only occasionally by brief moments of opportunism and achievement.

Indeed, so slow and rare is strategic change that Mintzberg and Waters (1985) suggest that we are at risk of seriously exaggerating its importance. According to them, organizations are characterized more by continuities than changes. Whether analysing the German car manufacturer Volkswagen (Mintzberg 1978) or the Canadian retailer Steinbergs (Mintzberg and Waters 1985), over the perspective of several decades the most striking element about their strategies is their essential stability. Policy details may change, but the core strategy remains basically intact over long stretches of time. Top management's task emerges as more managing continuity than implementing strategic change.

This clinging to the core strategy, rather than making constant adjustments according to changes in the environment, may actually best serve the global performance of the organization, even if it results in local inefficiencies. With the typical Processual emphasis on complexity, Miller (1982) characterizes organizations as developing over time into closely interrelated 'gestalts', all their elements mutually supporting and creating a coherent whole. To tinker with any of these elements, even on the edges, risks disturbing the internal equilibrium and setting off a degenerative collapse of the organizational gestalt. The costs of this gestalt collapse, and the difficulty of developing a new gestalt, may be far greater than the gains likely from periodic adjustments to small changes in the environment.

Although coming from the same Processual background, Miller's (1982) conclusion is therefore different from Pettigrew's (1985). They both agree that strategic change is hard; but precisely because of this Miller concludes that, rather than undertaking a continuous process of incremental advances, change should be held back until sufficient pressure has gathered for complete revolution.

> *Organizations often behave like sluggish thermostats. They must delay changing their structure until an important crisis develops. By then, quantum or revolutionary change may be required to re-establish harmony among many aspects of structure and environment.*

> (1982: 148)

For Miller, it is better to engage in episodic revolutions than to persevere through incremental evolution.

Of course, there is a Systemic perspective too on the relative appropriateness of revolutionary and incremental change. Countries differ in the density of their social and institutional environments. Germany and Japan are characterized by networks of relationships and mutual commitments. Anglo-Saxon societies are more individualistic and hard-headed. These different contexts have substantial implications for the kinds of change that are feasible. Lehrer and Darbishire (1999) compare long-run changes at Deutsche Telekom and Lufthansa, on the one hand, and British Telecom and British Airways on the other. In the 1960s and early 1970s, the German companies were relatively successful, harnessing their respect for technology and their consensual management styles to the incremental learning required of that slow-moving period. The British companies, meanwhile, were too locked-in to adversarial labour relations and stable financial returns to match the Germans. However, when rapid technological change combined with deregulation and increasing competition from the 1980s onwards, it was British Telecom and British Airways that took the lead. Here the decisive, low commitment and financially oriented management style of the British was initially the most successful in achieving the revolutionary changes required. Deutsche Telekom and Lufthansa caught up with the scale of change only in the 1990s. In other words, the pace and patterns of organizational change vary according to national context. But in neither Germanic nor Anglo-Saxon systems was business able perfectly to match organizational change with environmental change: the British failed to cope with incremental learning, the Germans with radical transformation.

The conclusion drawn by Mintzberg and Waters (1985) is a sobering one. The Classical approach misleads in its expectations of change – exaggerating both its importance and its ease. Classical planning mechanisms, with their annual strategy reviews, build in presumptions of change where none need be necessary. The training of the typical MBA, presented with case after case of organizational crises apparently demanding incisive action, cultivates an interventionist style of management that can create more problems than it solves. For Mintzberg and Waters (1985), the Classically trained MBA is a professional meddler in strategy, oversensitive to strategic issues, impulsive in his or her solutions. Their advice is: if it ain't broke, don't fix it.

Conclusions

The message of the Classical and Evolutionary schools is clear: change organizational structures to match changes in organizational strategies. Donaldson's (1987) statistical analysis of the correlation between performance and appropriate structure amongst large American corporations certainly confirmed the financial logic of this argument: diversified firms with multidivisional structures and non-diversified firms with functional structures performed better in terms of profit margin and return on investment growth than their mismatched peers. In the United States at least, fitting structure to strategy pays.

But for the Processualists, this is all too glib: the relationship between strategy and structure is not that simple and, anyway, changing anything is never going to be easy. The Processualist approach to change is more cautious. Following Miller (1982), it may sometimes be best to delay change, putting up with some local inefficiencies, rather than to risk unravelling the whole intricately interwoven gestalt of the organization by some ill-judged tinkering. If change is to be undertaken, then the Processual advice is usually to be modest in your expectations. Organizations do not change simply by decree. Achieving strategic change is likely to be a patient process of coaching, bargaining and manoeuvre.

Evolutionists are perfectly prepared to accept the difficulties of organizational change, but their conclusion is more brutal. In today's competitive world, there is no time for Processual procrastination. Use markets to compel change and carry it through. If managers will not change, change the managers; if the organization does not adapt, sell it and buy another one.

7 Does it matter?

For years I thought that what was good for our
country was good for General Motors and vice versa.
The difference did not exist. Our company is too big.
It goes with the welfare of the country.

(Charles Wilson, President of General Motors, 1951)

What's wrong with General Motors is wrong
with America.

(Kanter 1983: 313)

Introduction

Charles Wilson's proud certainty, and Kanter's (1983) critical inversion, link the two themes of this final chapter – implications both for managerial strategy and for government policy. We argue that the differences between the four basic approaches to strategy do matter. With their different perspectives on both human action and environments, they provide radically opposed recommendations for managers and governments alike.

General Motors has been at the centre of this book. Under Alfred Sloan, this great American manufacturing company developed for the first time both the distinct concept of strategy and the tools to implement it. With the help of disciples such as Ansoff, Chandler and Drucker, Sloan's Classical model of strategy has been enormously influential. Kanter's accusation is that this model, over the long term, has served neither the company nor America well.

There are other models of strategy though. On offer too are the invigorating ruthlessness of the Evolutionists, the modest pragmatism of the Processualists and the social relativism of the Systemicists. It is time to choose. First, which offers the most plausible recommendations for managerial action? Second – because firm strategies and national economic performance are so closely linked – which provides the most effective model for national industrial policy?

Managerial consequences

This book has dealt with four very different perspectives on strategy – Classical, Evolutionary, Processual and Systemic. Each of these is based on widely varying assumptions about the processes and outcomes of strategy, and each has quite opposite implications for managerial action. All four approaches remain areas of lively insightful scholarship and all are able to heap formidable bodies of evidence on their side. These divisions leave the practising manager with some hard choices.

Certainty is stolen away from every side. Classical confidence in analysis, order and control is undermined by Processual scepticism about human cognition, rationality and flexibility. The incrementalist learning of the Processualists is challenged in turn by the impatient markets of the Evolutionists. But even Evolutionary markets can be bucked if, as Systemic analysts of social systems allege, the state is persuaded to intervene.

Faced with these oppositions, for every manager the strategy-making process starts with a fundamental strategic choice: which theoretical picture of human activity and environment fits most closely with his or her own view of the world, his or her personal 'theory of action' (Argyris 1977). Is there sufficient access to information, sufficient capacity to analyse, sufficient organizational control and sufficient environmental certainty to make it worthwhile to invest time and energy in the rigours of Classical strategy-making? If all these conditions exist, then the Classical textbooks are fulsome in their advice. Strategic visions should project long into the future, inspiring the troops while never wavering from the bottom-line. Top managers should decide their strategies with all the cool objectivity of formulae and matrices, undistracted by the details of operations. Declining businesses should be smoothly replaced by market-led innovation and portfolio-guided diversification. Structures should always follow strategies.

Or rather is the environment as ruthlessly competitive and as unpredictably fluid as the Evolutionists claim? If so, the best resort is to abandon grand strategy and concentrate on operational efficiency. Long-range planning is a futile diversion from the pressing task of day-to-day survival. Anyway, textbook techniques are too widely available to give any competitive advantage. Evolutionists are hard-headed. Growth strategies of diversification and internalization must always be qualified by the humdrum criterion of transaction costs. If someone offers to do something cheaper than you yourself are doing it, drop the activity and just buy it in. Keep the organization sharp by letting everyone know that there are plenty of substitutes in the market-place – no person or activity is indispensable. Markets are too competitive to tolerate the inefficient, the slow or the deadweight. They are too unpredictable for narrowly spread bets. In short, the Evolutionists conclude, the best you can do in this tough uncertain world is to keep your costs low and your options open.

Or perhaps both markets and organizations are inherently imperfect, so that neither Classical precision nor Evolutionary ruthlessness are really appropriate. If markets do not work perfectly, then Processualists advise some respect for organizational integrity. The skills an organization embodies are not to be bought and sold freely on the market, but need to be cherished and cultivated as the unreproducible sources of sustainable advantage. True, organizations are slow to learn and politically conservative, but there is no need for the urgent surgery demanded by the Evolutionists. Markets are typically quite tolerant of lags in adaptation and may even reward those who do not embroil themselves in endless change. Likewise, the Classical obsession with formal techniques simply distracts managers from what really matters in strategy. The long reports of Classical planning are doomed to fall into the Processual 'garbage can' of organizational inertia. Anyway, real understanding does not come from the elevated analyses of flighty MBAs, but from the intimate knowledge of those who have made their lives in the business. Effective implementation is the result not of top-down command, but of the deep involvement that allows learning and incrementalism. The Processual message, then, is to keep close to the action and to be modest in your management. Innovation is easily smothered by planning and direction; organizational structures control the strategists as much as the other way round; change does not come to order, but by coaxing, coaching and compromise.

But finally none of these three perspectives on the world may satisfy. Systemic theory offers a fourth view. The techniques of Classical strategy evolved in the very peculiar conditions of American big business earlier this century, and even here their value may have been as much ideological as technical. In so far as Classical techniques have failed to deliver success on their home ground, they are still less likely to do so elsewhere. None the less, Systemic theorists do not succumb to Evolutionary and Processual pessimism over our ability to plan our activities and manipulate our environments. Contra the Evolutionists, the market is not all-powerful; contra the Processualists, apparently foolish or perverse behaviour may be perfectly rational when seen in context. The sociological imagination prompts a search for other sources of power in the environment, other rationalities for action. Thus the Systemic perspective points to the resources of state policy, cultural legitimacy and educational elitism; it illuminates the drives of managerial imperialism, professional self-promotion and class reproduction. Strategies of internationalization need not rely just on capitalist resources; they may draw on state subsidy and support. Strategies of diversification and divisionalization may have other advantages than just profit maximization; they offer top management power, security and prestige.

In the politics of organizational careers and decision-making, the Systemic perspective arms managers with sardonic self-awareness. Getting ahead involves not just merit, but also social conformity. Getting the right decisions can depend less on the content of formal analyses, more on the display of Classical rationality. Sociologically sensitive and just a little bit cynical, the Systemic manager is just as confident as the Classicist in plotting her future. The difference is that she secures her advance by drawing on a much more catholic range of social resources, and manipulates them with far greater sophistication.

These are four starkly different perspectives, but it is the Systemic sensibility that helps us finally to choose. For the Systemic strategist, effectiveness depends upon understanding context and playing by local rules. Sometimes Classical planning can deliver the goods. Yet sometimes the sheer ferocity or unpredictability of markets will drive us towards the Evolutionary camp. Other times, we will find that organizations are too sticky to bend to simple plans, or that the key resources on which competitive advantage rely are too embedded for detached manipulation from afar. There is no one best way. The key is to match strategy to market, organizational and social environments. As Figure 7.1 summarizes, Classical planning may have its place – but so too do Evolutionary, Processual and Systemic approaches.

Figure 7.1 **Different contexts for strategy**

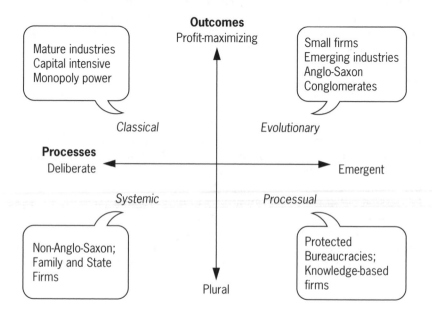

The Classical approach is most relevant in mature, stable and relatively predictable environments. There, at least, plans stand a chance of capturing the future. Where capital investments are large and lumpy, incrementalism is impractical and decisions require justification (Goold and Campbell 1987). Monopolists too may have enough power over their markets to ensure that their plans become true. Evolutionists, of course, warn that markets are prone to 'de-maturity', as sudden bursts of innovation break out or new entrants break in. This was the classic fate of the American automobile manufacturers in the 1970s (Abernathy and Clark 1985). In new or de-maturing industries, where many small firms still compete in the absence of market power, then the most reliable advice is the Evolutionary focus on low costs and spread bets. Equally, a preference for economy and an aversion towards risk are the characteristics most likely to promote survival for business managers in the ruthless selection environment of an Anglo-Saxon conglomerate. But even in more tolerant environments, Classical planning may be futile or ineffective. Processual approaches fit protected bureaucracies, especially public-sector or quasi-privatized agencies, which often have both the size and complexity of objectives to make of strategy a series of creeping but necessary compromises. Knowledge-based firms too, with powerful professions or deeply embedded competencies, are more effectively driven bottom-up rather than top-down. Such 'adhocracies' have the potential to muddle through over long periods of time and, accidentally or not, pretty profitably too (Mintzberg 1979). Finally, the Systemic perspective calls for clear diagnosis of local operating logics. In this respect, the Systemic approach to strategy does not give up on rational response; rather it recognizes the many rationalities that strategists may play by. Where the context demands obedience to textbook norms of rational profit-maximization, it is good advice to follow Classical rules – or at least to seem to.

National policy consequences

Chapter 1 identified the different growth rates of the two main competing forms of capitalism – the communitarian and incrementalist capitalism associated with Germany and Japan, against the market-dominated, individualistic capitalism of the United States and the United Kingdom. Neither form of capitalism seems to have delivered consistently superior rates of growth over the last four decades and neither is likely to do so permanently in the future. However, different rates of growth naturally stimulate questions about what governments can do to encourage faster economic development. With business at the heart of economic development, the four models of strategy have important implications for national policy initiatives as well. Of course, the models do not agree. Evolutionary and Processual accounts are sceptical of big government interventions, warning policy-makers to stand back and not to spoil emergent economic successes. Classical and Systemic approaches are more confident in deliberate action, but the Classical instinct is to make existing systems work better, the Systemic is towards quite radical social and institutional change.

The Classical approach to national economic performance is characteristically rooted in individualism and rationalism. Faith in both the perfectability of humankind and the stimulus of profit lead Classicists to rest their hopes on change at the level of the enterprise. National economic performance is simply the aggregate competitiveness of all the individual businesses that make up the economy. If national economies falter, then it is the responsibility of managers to better their own performance – to improve quality, to act globally, to learn flexibility, to think long term (cf. Dertouzos *et al.* 1989). Richard Nelson (1992) has termed this the 'pulling up management's socks' approach.

In short, the Classical solution to relative economic decline is to become cleverer. With their directive role in business life, the focus is on management education. Baruch and Peiperl (1999) estimate that the United States, with a managerial workforce of about 15 million, requires about half a million MBA graduates a year, just to replace those managers who are retiring. The American business schools produce only 75,000 new

MBA graduates annually. The United Kingdom too appears to face a chronic MBA deficit. According to the same authors, the United Kingdom's two million or so managerial workforce needs about 75,000 MBA graduates a year, against a total number actually produced around 10,000. The result of the United Kingdom's under-investment in management education is to reinforce the characteristic shambolic and amateurish nature of British managerial elites. Storey and Sisson (1990: 63) observe:

> *few British managers have had the opportunity to be exposed, in any serious and sustained way, to the actuality of formal planning processes. In the British context, planning, for too many managers, simply means budgeting.*
>
> (1990: 63)

A good deal of the British economic problem would be solved if only managers could be taught to plan as the Classical textbooks tell them to.

From the Classical perspective, then, failing economies need more MBAs. Witness the travails of Japan, where the first MBA programme started only in 1978, at Keio University (Ishida 1997). By the late 1990s, the expansion of MBA programmes was an urgent government priority, with Prime Minister Keizo Obuchi himself pressing the two traditional elite universities of Tokyo and Kyoto to launch into business education (*The Economist*, 13 November 1999). The same enthusiasm for business education as a motor for economic reform has been evident in the transition economies of Eastern Europe, where American business schools have been particularly prominent, recalling the Marshall Plan in post-war Western Europe forty years before (Gobeli *et al.* 1998). A major challenge for business educators has been to address the ethical consequences of bringing state-power and free-market opportunism into sudden collision (Sexty 1998). For many, a condition for creating prosperity in the transition economies is the establishment of a managerial class operating according to both the professional and the ethical norms of Western business schools. The MBA has a moral mission too.

Wealth creation and professional ethics are sometimes not easily aligned. In Russia at least, personal success has often required playing by quite different rules to those of the MBA (see 'Russian oligarchs'). Freeland (2000: 111) observes: 'Western business schools tell their students that the secret of success is to know your customers. In the late Soviet Union it was to know your apparatchiks'. The Systemic warning is not to put too much faith in Classical professional management out of context. Henry Mintzberg (1996b) is just as scornful of the value of MBA education, but from a Processual perspective. The trouble with the MBA is that it licenses fast careers in which nobody gets their hands dirty learning about the nitty-gritty of real business life. The result is too many managers inclined towards lofty analysis, failing to get to grips with a complex and messy reality. Rather than extending the MBA model, Mintzberg (1996b: 67) declares: 'It is time to close down conventional MBA programmes'.

As the arch-Processualist, Mintzberg is sceptical of top-down, deliberate programmes of change. The Processual model of economic development stresses the bottom-up cultivation of historical and geographical accident. Here a reformed Michael Porter (1990, 1998) comes strikingly

Russian oligarchs

The careers of the richest and most powerful men of Russia have been made without the benefits of MBA classes in finance, marketing and ethics. Consider three:

1. In the late 1990s, Vladimir Potanin's Oneximbank empire was estimated as controlling 10 per cent of Russia's GDP. Potanin started out as an elite Soviet bureaucrat in the Ministry of Foreign Trade. He got his big break in 1992 by using his nomenklatura contacts to obtain control over the accounts of the collapsing state-owned bank, the International Bank of Economic Cooperation. As Potanin admits: 'Basically, they gave us $300m'.

2. In 1997, Boris Berezovsky was named by *Forbes* magazine as the ninth most powerful entrepreneur in the world. Amongst many assets, he controlled the output of the largest car factory in the world, the Togliatti Lada car-plant. More important, he also had the ear of the President Boris Yeltsin and his family. Having secured the rights to publish Yeltsin's memoirs in 1993, Berezovsky was able to furnish the President a steady supply of generous royalty cheques. Control over Aeroflot and the state television station followed.

3. Vladimir Gusinsky started out selling copper bracelets, securing the necessary raw materials by trading bottles of vodka for copper wire off broken-down trams. By the early 1990s, his friendship with the mayor of Moscow was winning lucrative construction contracts for his company, conveniently operating from a headquarters in Moscow city hall. By the late 1990s, Gusinsky controlled the dominant media empire in Russia, the Most Group. Gusinsky is quite frank: 'I cannot say I am an absolutely honest man'.

Source: Freeland 2000.

into belated agreement with the advocates of emergence. Porter (1990) now stresses how successful industries tend to develop within local 'clusters' of mutually supporting factors. Successful clusters include the semiconductor cluster of Silicon Valley, the media cluster of Hollywood, the electronics cluster around the Hsinchu Science Park in Taiwan, the leather cluster in North Italy, the engineering cluster of Baden-Wurttemburg, and the motor sport cluster in the Thames Valley (see 'Racing accidents'). All these clusters bring together into a concentrated location the four key elements of Porter's (1990) 'diamond' model of economic development: appropriate demand conditions (such as sophisticated customers); good factor conditions (particularly a supply of necessary skills); related and supporting industries (providing a broad infrastructure); and finally firm strategies and rivalry (ensuring competitiveness). But these clusters are rarely the product of strategic design.

Racing accidents

Nine out of ten of the world's Formula One racing cars, and about three-quar-ters of the American Indy Racing League vehicles, are designed and produced within a 50 mile radius of Oxfordshire, in Southern England. Even Ferrari moved its design and manufacture to the region in the 1990s.

This successful motor sport cluster is the result of many self-reinforcing accidents. Before the Second World War, there were no totally British designed and built cars competing in continental European Grand Prix races, and in the early post-war period, it was the Italians and Germans who dominated. But the Germans were knocked-out by the 1955 accident at Le Mans, when a Mercedes span out of control to kill 183 spectators, resulting in the withdrawal of the Mercedes team from motor sport. The Italians were set-back by a change in the Formula One rules to require each competitor to produce its own chassis, meaning that no single manufacturer could dominate the grid, as Ferrari had done. Small British teams such as Cooper and Brabham were given a chance.

The south of England was also helped by the legacy of the Second World War. There were many redundant airfields in the region, providing cheap test-ing grounds. There were also many aeronautical engineering research insti-tutes nearby, such as Imperial College and Farnborough. As technology changed in racing during the 1960s and 1970s, aerospace skills became criti-cal, rather than the traditional automobile engineering at which the Italians were strong. The British seized the advantage with their superior knowledge in aerodynamics, aluminium and composite materials, and high performance breaking and clutch systems. A final factor in British success was the 1965 UK ban on cigarette advertising on television. British teams such as Lotus gained massive sponsorship from tobacco companies eager to plant their logos prominently on the side of successful racing cars.

Source: *The Economist*, 15 November 1997; Pinch and Henry 1999.

The clustering model of economic development builds upon the typical elements of the Processual model – emergent logics and sticky resources. Thus the enduring success of particular clusters relies upon the stickiness of the critical inputs: the people who carry critical skills and knowledge tend to prefer to pursue their careers in one location; the exchange of knowledge by which wealth is multiplied is better achieved by those who live and work side-by-side. Knowledge and people prosper with the trust and co-operation born of familiarity and proximity. Clusters, moreover, tend to emerge first by accident and then by cumulative processes of 'lock-in'. Kenney and von Burg (1999) trace the origins of Silicon Valley to the reluc-tance of East Coast financiers to provide William Shockley, co-inventor of the transistor at Bell Laboratories, with the necessary venture capital to exploit his new device. By chance, it was finally a Los Angeles firm that sup-plied the capital and Shockley moved to Palo Alto. By chance too, Shockley proved a bad manager, and all eight of his initial hires resigned within two years to found Fairchild Semiconductor. Fairchild in turn span out Intel, LSI Logic, National Semiconductor, AMD and Signetics, amongst many others. The virtuous circle of Silicon Valley was established.

This Processual reliance on the local and emergent implies a cautious and highly sensitive approach to economic development. The role of government is to support existing processes on the ground and not to get in the way. Government is the nurse, not the parent, of new industries. There are good Systemic grounds for thinking this may be too fatalistic: the conditions for new clusters can be created deliberately by firms and governments working together in full knowledge of the necessary conditions for economic success (Saxenian 1999). Evolutionary theory differs from the other end of the spectrum. Processualists mistake Silicon Valley for a seed-bed of cosy relationships; in fact it is a hot-bed of ruthless competition (Gilder 1988). Tender-hearted nursing is not what industry needs for continued dynamism.

The Evolutionary route to economic growth is to rely on markets and entrepreneurship. Unlike the Classicists, the Evolutionists have little faith in the professional managers of large corporations to plan the effective and unselfish deployment of the economic assets. Large corporations should be subject to the ruthless disciplines of the market for corporate control (Jensen 1989). The beauty-contests of contested take-overs sift out the incompetent, the self-interested and the decaying. The simple threat of take-over and break-up pressurizes managers in maturing industries to release cash through dividends so that shareholders can reinvest in new, higher growth industries. In this view, the roots of today's stagnation in Japan can be traced back to the Japanese refusal to accept the competition-based capital markets introduced by the American occupation forces during the late 1940s. Helweg (2000), a Project Director in the US Council on Foreign Relations, applauds the failures of Sanyo Bank, Hokkaido Takushoku Bank and Yamaichi Securities: the traditional bank-centred *keiretsu* are far too cosy. The dynamic, unsentimental capitalism of the United States offers Japan the best way forward.

The Grameen Bank

The Grameen Bank (the rural bank in Bengali) started as a result of the frustration of economist Muhammad Yunus at the repeated failures of traditional and centralized aid programmes in Bangladesh. Starting in 1976, he began to lend tiny amounts of capital to help the very poor break out of the dependency relationships into which poverty had trapped them. Thus he lent to village women making bamboo stools the money they needed to buy the bamboo, so releasing them from costly dependence on exorbitant money-lenders. With cheaper and more systematic borrowing, the village women were suddenly able to make a reasonable living for the first time.

The Grameen Bank now has $2 billion in loans, with an average loan size of just $160. Interest rates are not particularly cheap – 16–20 per cent – and about one quarter of loans are not repaid. Nevertheless, the Bank is helping two million people in 35,000 villages. Many of these people had been side-lined in previous aid programmes: 94 per cent of borrowers are women. The Bank is also helping to link Bangladeshi villages to the rest of the world through mobile phones and the Internet. Fifty-two countries are now imitating these microcredit initiatives, including the United States.

The Grameen Bank does not get involved in education and training for its clients. According to Yunus, with a Darwinian faith in survivors: 'I believe that all human beings have an innate skill. I call it the survival skill. The fact that the poor are alive is proof of their ability'.

Sources: Stallings 1999; *Independent on Sunday*, 5 May 1996;
www.grameen-info.org

Critical to the Evolutionary view on economic policy is respect for the high-earning, high risk-taking entrepreneur. By contrast with Classical MBAs, these entrepreneurs are often not overburdened with sophisticated education. Gilder (1992) notes that of the *Forbes* 400 most wealthy people in America, more than half created their fortunes through entrepreneurship, one quarter never went to college, and a further sixty failed to graduate. Harvard drop-out Bill Gates is the model. But entrepreneurship in this view is not necessarily just about creating the super-rich. The Evolutionary enthusiasm for entrepreneurship can also be put to the service of the very poor. The microcredit movement stimulated by the Grameen Bank of Bangladesh has used semi-commercial processes to provide tiny amounts of finance to help the small business activities of the poor around the world. Failure rates are high, but that is allowed for in the interest rates. In any case, microcredit reaches people ignored by the Classical state-led initiatives of traditional development. Rather than relying on government bureaucrats or the dependency of aid, microcredit allows the poor to work their way out of poverty for themselves (see 'The Grameen Bank').

To an extent, the Evolutionary enthusiasts for market disciplines and entrepreneurial initiative are promoting wholesale changes of social and economic systems. Helweg's (2000) delight at Japanese banking failures is the thin end of a wedge challenging the traditional communitarian social and economic organization of Japan as a whole. The Grameen Bank's empowerment of women borrowers undermines ancient power structures within Bangladeshi villages. These are not the kinds of change that go unchallenged. Indeed, the longstanding criticism of reliance upon competitive markets is that they disrupt social communities and promote myopic opportunism. For a long time, the capital markets of the United States and the United Kingdom have been seen as the problem, promoting economic 'short-termism' and labour market antagonism. According to the charge-sheet, the Anglo-Saxon systems are too reliant upon hostile takeovers for the disciplining of management, price their capital more highly than in competitor countries, and allow their shareholders too easily to vote with their feet rather than to foster long-term relationships with their enterprises (Laverty 1997; Mayer 1997). The result has been inadequate investments in R&D, capital equipment and training, by comparison with Germany and Japan during the 1980s at least (Williams 1991; Crouch *et al.* 1999).

More recent economic history does not suggest that the Anglo-Saxon systems are unprepared to invest in the long-term: the boom in profitless Internet stocks at the turn-of-the-century suggests quite the reverse. Mayer (1997) discounts all the major charges of short-termism and suggests, with Evolutionary logic, that if change is needed to the system at all, then it is in the direction of still further removal of constraints on the freedom of markets and enterprise. Indeed, whereas once Systemic thinking saw the state as leading system-wide reforms (Cowling and Sawyer 1990), the dominant strand of thought now has been to promote market-led changes to economic and social systems.

Table 7.1 **Control of publicly-traded companies in East Asia**

	No. of Corporations	Widely-held (%)	Family (%)	State (%)
Hong Kong	330	0.6	64.5	3.7
Indonesia	178	0.6	67.1	10.2
Korea	345	14.3	67.9	5.1
Malaysia	238	1.0	57.7	17.8
Philippines	120	1.7	41.3	3.6
Singapore	221	1.4	51.9	23.6
Taiwan	280	2.8	65.6	3.0

Source: Chong Nam *et al.* 1999.

The Asian Crisis of the late 1990s was widely blamed on the alleged 'crony capitalism' of powerful families and protective states that had grown up throughout the region. Table 7.1 shows that the proportions of companies under family or state control in a range of East Asian countries: typically between half and two-thirds of companies are under such control. With the slight exception of Korea, the proportion of widely held companies, more or less tradable in the manner of Anglo-Saxon companies, is negligible (remaining companies are generally under the control of financial institutions or other corporations). In the Philippines and Indonesia, more than one-sixth of market capitalization could be traced to the ultimate control of single families, the Ayalas and the Suhartos respectively (Chong Nam *et al.* 1999). The result in these Asian countries has been an economic system in which the efficient allocation of resources has been under no external market discipline. Conglomerates sprawled and debts ballooned without supervision or sanction. When the crisis finally came, much of the earlier Asian miracle was exposed as a house-of-cards, with businesses supporting each other in precarious pyramids of debt and shady deals.

Although closely connected to the Asian region economically, Anglo-Saxon Australia survived the Asian crisis well because of its superior system of corporate governance. For Andrew Cheng (1999), Chairman of the Hong Kong Securities and Futures Commission, the lesson is widespread reform of corporate governance. Asian corporations need more outside directors, more transparent accounting and tougher regulation. What is at stake in governance reform, however, is more than superficial corporate regulation. Corporate governance is intimately related to social, economic and political systems as wholes. The conservative Ayala family has been central to the political and economic development of the Philippines for more than two centuries (*Business Week*, 23 July 2000). Wealthy families have avoided transparency and accountability because it suited their private purposes – and they have been powerful enough to make the rules. The solution to Asia's problems involves, therefore, radical transformation of whole societies. The prescription from a Systemic perspective is that, for secure economic growth to be obtained, the powers of both dominant families and corrupt states must be radically reduced. There may be something to be said for the professional MBA and capital market disciplines after all.

Just as for questions of strategy at the level of the firm, therefore, the Classical, Processual, Evolutionary and Systemic perspectives offer competing prescriptions for national economic policy. The Classical prescription is to rely on better thinking and planning. The Processualists nurture developments from the bottom-up. Evolutionists stand back, hoping only to turn the winnowing processes of competitive markets to general advantage. Finally the Systemic perspective sees business strategy and economic performance as tightly linked to the social contexts in which they are embedded. Economic change means social and political change as well. Systemicists are believers in deliberate social engineering.

There can be no sure answer about which policy approach is best. At one level, these are political questions. At another level, they raise fundamental questions about our capacities and purposes as human beings. These are the terms of Figure 1.1: to what extent are we capable of managing ourselves deliberately, rather than subject to the irrational and the unforeseen; and what kinds of outcomes does the world allow for our activities, narrowly economistic or broad and plural? Again, there can be many answers to these questions. The point of this book is not to prescribe a single answer. Rather, the point is that our views on human capacities and purposes underpin our approaches to all kinds of strategy-making, whether at the level of the nation, the firm or even the individual. We can reasonably differ about our philosophical positions on these fundamental questions. But, whatever our positions, at least being clear about our underlying philosophies should make our strategies more coherent – and, hopefully, more effective. What you think strategy is certainly does matter.

N otes

1 What is strategy – and does it matter?

This book originated from a seminar paper, 'What is strategy – and does it matter? The case of industrial relations', given to the Industrial Relations Research Unit, University of Warwick, in June 1990. Helpful comments on the paper were given by Harry Scarborough, Paul Marginson and Steve Wood. The development of the book has benefited more generally from the stimulating atmosphere at Warwick, challenging MBA students and, especially, the patience of my wife, Maria.

1   This book largely confines itself to 'business' strategy, because the theoretical bases of the four basic perspectives on strategy, especially the Evolutionary perspective, draw heavily upon private-sector assumptions. This is not to say that the perspectives are inapplicable to the public sector. In particular, the Systemic sensitivity to sociological complexity and difference should be especially appropriate to the emergent quasi-privatized enterprises of recent years.

2   The term 'Anglo-Saxon' economies conventionally includes the United States, the United Kingdom, Canada, Australia and New Zealand. These countries share a bent towards free-market economics and historical links through British imperialism. The term is not intended to imply ethnic homogeneity.

2 Theories of strategy

1   For more on transaction costs see the sections on diversification and internationalization in Chapter 5.

2   On game theory, see the section on internationalization in Chapter 5.

3   Mintzberg's (1990) critique in fact refers more specifically to the 'design school', but Ansoff (1991) at least interpreted this as including all orthodox Classical thought. Certainly Mintzberg's premises – of which there are seven in all – apply quite broadly.

4   It is odd that Marxian critics of capitalist enterprise should generally accept Classical assumptions of rationality and effectiveness. Thus D. M. Gordon *et al.* (1982) give great credence to corporate planning, while Braverman (1974) has huge faith in the Taylorist separation of hand and brain, a close equivalent of Alfred Sloan's (1963) distinction between policy formulation and execution. See also the section on technology in Chapter 5.

5   Some recent 'evolutionary economists' have been less sanguine about the effectiveness of market forces and efficient outcomes: see Saviotti and Metcalfe (1991).

6   In fact, Peter Drucker (1973: 18) anticipated this analogy: 'The manager has to be a craftsman.'

4   Strategic choice

1   Clear introductions to these techniques are provided in G. Johnson and Scholes (1998), Grant (1991a) and many other textbooks.

2   'Option pricing' is a financial technique which values the options that a particular investment may open up for the future, as well as the revenue stream arising directly from the investment. The value of investments in research and development may lie almost entirely in the options they create. See 'Betting on the Future' (p. 59).

3   For the debate between the voluntaristic 'strategic choice' theories of corporate and human action and more deterministic perspectives, see Child (1972), whittington (1988) and D. C. Wilson (1992). The issues involved in this debate are not dealt with directly here.

4   Clear introductions to these and other Classical techniques are provided in G. Johnson and Scholes (1998), Dyson (1990) and Grant (1998).

5   McKiernan (1992), in another book in this series, provides an extensive discussion of the strengths and weaknesses of the Boston Consulting Group's matrix.

References

Abernathy, W. J. and Clark, K. B. (1985) 'Mapping the winds of creative destruction', *Research Policy* 14(1): 3–23.

Albert, M. (1991) *Capitalisme contre Capitalisme*, Paris: Editions de Seuil.

Alchian, A. A. (1950) 'Uncertainty, evolution and economic theory', *Journal of Political Economy* 58: 211–21.

Aldrich, H. E. (1979) *Organizations and Environments*, Englewood Cliffs, NJ: Prentice Hall.

Anchordoguy, M. (1990) 'A brief history of Japan's keiretsu', *Harvard Business Review* July–August: 58–9.

Ansoff, H. I. (1965) *Corporate Strategy*, Harmondsworth: Penguin.

—— (1991) 'Critique of Henry Mintzberg's "The Design School"', *Strategic Management Journal* 12: 449–61.

Aoki, M. (1990) 'Towards an economic model of the Japanese firm', *Journal of Economic Literature* 24 (March): 1–27.

Appignanesi, R. and Garratt, C. (1995) *Postmodernism for Beginners*, London: Icon.

Argyris, C. (1977) 'Double loop learning in organizations', *Harvard Business Review* September–October: 115–25.

—— (1991) 'Teaching smart people to learn', *Harvard Business Review* May–June: 99–109.

Armstrong, P. (1985) 'Changing management control strategies: the role of competition between accounting and other organisation professions', *Accounting, Organizations and Society* 10 (2): 129–48.

—— (1987) 'Engineers, management and trust', *Work, Employment and Society* l (4): 421–40.

—— (1991) 'Contradictions and social dynamics in the capitalist agency relationship', *Accounting, Organizations and Society* 18 (1): 1–25.

Arthur, W. B. (1989) 'Competing technologies, increasing returns and lock-in by historical events', *Economic Journal* 99: 116–31.

Asquith, P. (1983) 'Merger bids, uncertainty and stockholder returns', *Journal of Financial Economics* 11: 51–83.

Baden-Fuller, C. and Stopford, J. (1994) *Rejuvenating the Mature Business*, Boston, MA: Harvard Business School Press.

Ballance, R. H. (1987) *International Industry and Business*, London: Allen & Unwin.

Barnard, C. (1938) *The Functions of the Executive*, Boston, MA: Harvard University Press.

Bartlett, R. (1989) *Economics and Power*, Cambridge: Cambridge University Press.

Baruch, Y. and Pieperl, M. (1999) 'The impact of an MBA on graduate careers'. *Human Resource Management Journal* 10 (2): 69–89.

Barwise, P., Marsh, P. and Wensley, R. (1989) 'Must finance and strategy clash?', *Harvard Business Review* September–October: 85–90.

Bass, B. M. (1985) *Leadership and Performance Beyond Expectations*, New York: Free Press.

—— (1990) 'From transactional to transformational leadership: learning to share the vision', *Organizational Dynamics* 18 (3): 19–31.

Bauer, M. and Bertin-Mourot, B. (1996) *Vers un Modèle Européen de Dirigeants?*, Paris: CNRS.

Bauer, M. and Cohen, E. (1983) 'La fin des nouvelles classes: couches moyennes eclatées et société d'appareils', *Revue Francaise de Sociologie* 24 (2): 285–300.

Baumol, W. J. (1959) *Business Behaviour, Value and Growth*, New York: Harcourt, Brace & World.

Berle, A. A. and Means, G. C. (1967) *The Modern Corporation and Private Property* (originally published 1932), New York: Harvest.

Berners-Lee, T. (1999) *Weaving the Web*, London: Orion.

Bibeault, D. B. (1982) *Corporate Turnaround*, New York: McGraw-Hill.

Biggart, N. (1989) *Charismatic Capitalism*, Chicago, IL: University of Chicago Press.

Birley, S. (1990) 'Corporate strategy and the small firm', in D. Asch and C. Bowman (eds) *Readings in Strategic Management*, London: Macmillan.

Bourgeois, L. J. (1980) 'Performance and consensus', *Strategic Management Journal* l (July–September): 227–98.

Boyacigiller, N. and Adler, N. (1991) 'The parochial dinosaur: organization science in a global context', *Academy of Management Review* 16 (2): 262–90.

Boyd, B. K. (1991) 'Strategic planning and financial performance', *Journal of Management Studies* 28 (4): 353–74.

Bracker, J. (1980) 'The historical development of the strategic management concept', *Academy of Management Review* 5 (2): 219–24.

Bradley, M., Desai, A. and Kim, E. H. (1988) 'Synergistic gains from corporate acquisitions and their division between the stockholders of target and acquiring firms', *Journal of Financial Economics* 21: 3–40.

Braverman, H. (1974) *Labor and Monopoly Capitalism*, New York: Monthly Review Press.

Brealy, R. A. and Myers S. C. (1988) *Principles of Corporate Finance*, 3rd edn, New York: McGraw-Hill.

Brews, P. and Hunt, M. (1999) 'Learning to Plan and Planning to Learn: Resolving the Planning School/Learning School Debate', *Strategic Management Journal* 20 (10): 889–914.

Brown, S. and Eisenhardt, K. (1999) *Competing on the Edge: Strategy as Structured Chaos*, Boston: Harvard Business School Press.

Brownlie, D. T. (1987) 'The strategic management of technology: a new wave of market-led pragmatism or a return to product orientation?', *European Journal of Marketing* 21(9): 45–65.

Bruner, R. (1999) 'An analysis of value destruction and recovery in the alliance and proposed merger of Volvo and Renault', *Journal of Financial Economics* 51: 125–166.

Brunsson, N. (1989) The Organization of Hypocrisy, London: Wiley.

—— (1990) 'Deciding for responsibility and legitimation: alternative interpretation of organizational decision-making', *Accounting, Organizations and Society* 15 (1–2): 47–59.

Bruton, G. D., Lan, H. and Lu, Y. (2000) 'China's township and village enterprises: Kelon's competitive edge', *Academy of Management Executive* 14 (1): 19–30.

Burgelman, R. A. (1996) 'Intraorganizational ecology of strategy making and organizational adaptation: theory and field research', in J. Meindl, C. Stubbart and J. Porac (eds) *Cognition within and between Organizations*, Thousand Oaks, CA: Sage.

Buzzell, R. D. and Gale, B. T. (1987) *The PIMS Principles*, New York: Free Press.

Calas, M. B. and Smircich, L. (1991) 'Voicing seduction to silence leadership', *Organization Studies* 12 (4): 567–602.

Campbell, A., Devine, M. and Young, D. (1990) *A Sense of Mission*, London: Hutchinson.

Carr, C. and Tomkins, C. (1998) 'Context, culture and the role of the financial function in strategic decisions: a comparative analysis of Britain, Germany, the USA and Japan', *Management Accounting Research* 9 (2): 213–39.

Carr, C., Tomkins, C. and Bayliss, B. (1991) 'Strategic controllership – a case study approach', *Management Accounting Research* 2: 89–107.

Casson, M. (1987) *The Firm and the Market*, Oxford: Blackwell.

Caves, R. E. (1989) 'Mergers, takeovers and economic efficiency', *International Journal of Industrial Organization* 7: 151–74.

Castells, M. (1996) *The Rise of the Network Society*, Oxford: Blackwells.

Caves, R. E. (1989) 'Mergers, takeovers and economic efficiency', *International Journal of Industrial Organization* 7: 151–74.

Chandler, A. D. (1962) *Strategy and Structure. Chapters in the History of the American Industrial Enterprise*, Cambridge, MA: MIT Press.

—— (1977) *The Visible Hand: The Managerial Revolution in American Business*, Cambridge, MA: Harvard University Press.

—— (1990) *Scale and Scope: Dynamics of Industrial Capitalism*, Cambridge, MA: Harvard University Press.

Channon, D. (1973) *The Strategy and Structure of British Enterprise*, Cambridge, MA: Harvard University Press.

Child, J. (1972) 'Organisational structure, environment and performance: the role of strategic choice', *Sociology* 6: 1–22.

Chong Nam, I., Kang, Y. and Kim, J-K (1999) *Comparative Corporate Governance Trends in Asia*, Paris: Organisation for Economic Co-operation and Development.

Clarke, W. and Herbst, J. (1996) 'Somalia and the future of humanitarian intervention', *Foreign Affairs* 75 (2): 70–80.

Cohen, E. (1988) 'Formation, modéles d'action et performance de l'élite industrielle', *Sociologie du Travail* 4: 587–611.

Cohen, M. D., March, J. G. and Olsen, J. P. (1972) 'A garbage can model of organizational choice', *Administrative Science Quarterly* 17: 1–25.

—— (1976) 'People, problems, solutions and the ambiguity of relevance', in J. March and J. Olsen (eds) *Ambiguity and Choice in Organisations*, Bergen: Universitetsforlaget.

Collins, J. C. and Porras, J. I. (1991) 'Organizational vision and visionary organizations', *California Management Review* Fall: 30–53.

Collis, D. (1991) 'A resource-based analysis of global competition: the case of the bearings industry', *Strategic Management Journal* 12: 49–68.

Collis, D. J. and Montgomery, C. A. (1995) 'Competing on resources: strategy in the 1990s', *Harvard Business Review*, July–August: 119–28.

Conner, K. and Prahalad, C.K. (1996) 'A resource-based theory of the firm: knowledge versus opportunism', *Organization Science* 7 (5): 477–501.

Cooper, R. G. and Brentani, U. (1981) 'Project new prod: factors in new product success', *European Journal of Marketing* 14 (5–6): 277–92.

Cooper, R. G. and Brentani, U. (1991) 'New industrial financial services: what distinguishes the winners', *Journal of Product Innovation Management* 8: 75–90.

Cowling, K. (1990) 'A new industrial strategy: preparing Europe for the turn of the century', *International Journal of Industrial Organization* 8: 163–83.

Cowling, K. and Sawyer, M. (1990) 'Merger and monopoly policy', in K. Cowling and R. Sugden (eds) *A New Economic Policy for Britain*, Manchester: Manchester University Press.

Cowling K. and Sugden, R. (1987) *Transnational Monopoly Capitalism*, Brighton: Wheatsheaf.

Crouch, C. Finegold, D. and Sako, M. (1999) *Are Skills the Answer?*, Oxford: Oxford University Press.

Cusumano, M. A. and Selby, R. W. (1996) *Microsoft Secrets*, London: Harper Collins.

Cusumano, M. A. and Yoffie, D. B. (1998) *Competing on Internet Time: Lessons from Netscape and its Battle with Microsoft*, New York: Free Press.

Cyert, R. M. and March, J. G. (1956) 'Organisational factors in the theory of monopoly', *Quarterly Journal of Economics* 70 (1): 44–64.

—— (1963) *A Behavioural Theory of the Firm*, Englewood Cliffs, NJ:Prentice Hall.

Czarniawska-Joerges, B. and Wolff, R. (1991) 'Leaders on and off the organisational stage', *Organization Studies* 12 (4): 529–46.

Dahrendorf, R. (1959) *Class and Class Conflict in Industrial Society*, London: Routledge & Kegan Paul.

Daily, C., Certo, S. and Dalton, D. (1999) 'A decade of corporate women: progress in the boardroom, none in the executive suite', *Strategic Management Journal* 20: 93–9.

Datta, D., Rajagopalan, N. and Rasheed, A. (1991) 'Diversification and performance: a critical review', *Journal of Management Studies* 28 (5): 529–57.

David, P. A. (1985) 'Clio and the economics of QWERTY', *Economic History* 75 (2): 332–7.

Davis, G. (1991) 'Agents without principles? The spread of the poison pill through the intercorporate network', *Administrative Science Quarterly* 36 (4): 583–614.

Davis, G., Dieljman, K. and Tinsely, C. (1994) 'The decline and fall of the conglomerate firm in the 1980s: the deinstitutionalization of an organizational form', *American Sociological Review* 59: 547–70.

De Geus (1988) 'Planning as learning', *Harvard Business Review* March–April: 70–4.

DeLamarter, R. (1986) *Big Blue: IBM's Use and Abuse of Power*, London: Macmillan.

Derdack, T. (1988) *International Directory of Company Histories*, Chicago, IL: St. James Press.

Dess, G. (1987) 'Consensus on strategy formulation and organizational performance: competitors in a fragmented industry', *Strategic Management Journal* 8: 259–77.

De Wit, B. and Meyer, R. (1999) *Strategy Synthesis*, London: Thomson.

DiMaggio, P. and Powell, W. W. (1983) 'The iron cage revisited: institutional isomorphism and collective rationality in organizational fields', *American Sociological Review* 48: 147–80.

Dixit, A. K. and Nabeluff, B. J. (1991) *Thinking Strategically: the Competitive Edge in Business, Politics and Everyday Life*, New York: W. W. Norton.

Donaldson, L. (1987) 'Strategy and structural adjustment to regain fit and performance: in defence of contingency theory', *Journal of Management Studies* 24 (1): 1–24.

Dore, R. (1983) 'Goodwill and the spirit of market capitalism', *British Journal of Sociology* 34: 459–82.

Dosi, G. (1988) 'Sources, procedures and microeconomic effects of innovation', *Journal of Economic Literature* 26: 1120–71.

Downes, L. and Mui, C. (1998) 'The end of strategy', *Strategy & Leadership* 26 (5): 4–10.

Doyle, P. (1990) 'Britain's left-and-right handed companies', *MBA Review* 2 (1): 5–8.

Doyle, P., Saunders, J. and Wong, V. (1992) 'Competition in global markets: a case study of American and Japanese competition in the British market', *Journal of International Business Studies*, 23 (3): 419–443.

Drucker, P. F. (1946) *The Concept of the Corporation*, London: Heinemann.

—— (1947) *Big Business*, London: Heinemann.

—— (1973) *Management: Tasks, Responsibilities, Practices*, London: Heinemann.

Du Boff, R. B. and Herman, E. S. (1980) 'A. Chandler's *New Business History*: a review', *Politics and Society* 10 (1): 87–110.

Dunning, J. H. (1988) *Explaining International Production*, London: HarperCollins.

Dyas, G. P. And Thanheiser, H. T. (1976) *The Emerging European Enterprise*, London: Macmillan.

Dyer, J. and Nobeoko, K. (2000) 'Creating and managing a high performance knowledge-sharing network: the Toyota case', *Strategic Management Journal* 21 (3): 345–67.

Dyson, R. (1990) *Strategic Planning: Models and Analytical Techniques*, Chichester: Wiley.

The Economist (1993) 'Eenie, meenie, minie, mo . . .' 20 March, 106.

Einhorn, H. J. and Hogarth, R. M. (1988) 'Behavioural decision theory: process of judgement and choice', in D. E. Bell, H. Raiffa and A. Tversky (eds) *Decision-making: Descriptive Normative and Prescriptive Interactions*, Cambridge: Cambridge University Press.

Eisenhardt, K. M. (1989) 'Agency theory: an assessment and review', *Academy of Management Review* 14 (1): 57–74.

Espeland, W. N. and Hirsch, P. M. (1990) 'Ownership changes, accounting practice and the redefinition of the corporation', *Accounting, Organizations and Society* 15 (1–2): 77–96.

Fama, E. F. (1980) 'Agency problems and the theory of the firm', *Journal of Political Economy* 88 (2): 288–307.

Feldman, M. S. and March, J. G. (1981) 'Information in organizations as signal and symbol', *Administrative Science Quarterly* 26: 171–86.

Ferguson, C. H. (1990) 'Computers and the coming of the U.S. *keiretsu*', *Harvard Business Review* July–August: 55–70.

Fligstein, N. (1987) 'Intraorganisational power struggles: the rise of finance personnel to top leadership in large corporations, 1919–1979', *American Sociology Reveiw* 52: 44–58.

—— (1990) *The Transformation of Corporate Control*, Cambridge, MA: Harvard University Press.

Flowers, E. B. (1976) Oligopolistic reaction in European direct investment in the United States', *Journal of International Business Studies* Fall–Winter: 43–55.

Francis, A. (1983) 'Markets and hierarchies: efficiency or domination?', in A. Francis, J. Turk and P. William (eds) *Power, Efficiency and Institutions*, London: Heinemann.

Freeland, C. (2000) *Sale of the Century: the Inside Story of Russia's Second Revolution*, London: Little Brown.

Freeman, C., Sharp, M. and Walker, W. (eds) (1991) *Technology and the Future of Europe*, London: Pinter.

Friedman, M. (1953) 'The methodology of positive economics', in M. Friedman, *Essays in Positive Economics*, Chicago, IL: University of Chicago Press.

Gall, L. (1995) *The Deutsche Bank, 1870–1995*, London: Weidenfeld and Nicholson.

Gestrin, M. V., Knight, R. F. and Rugman, P. M. (2000) *Templeton Global Performance Index 2000*, Oxford: Templeton College, University of Oxford.

Ghoshal, S. and Bartlett, C. (1995) 'Changing the role of top management: beyond structure to process', *Harvard Business Review* January–February: 86–96.

Ghoshal, S., Bartlett, C. and Moran, P. (1999) 'A new manifesto for management', *Sloan Management Review* Spring: 9–20.

Gilder, G. (1988) 'The revitalization of everything: the law of the microcosm', *Harvard Business Review* March–April: 49–61.

—— (1992) 'The Enigma of Entrepreneurial Wealth', *Inc.* 14 (10): 161–9.

Gobeli, D., Przybylowski, K. and Rudelius, W. (1998) 'Customizing management training in central and eastern Europe: mini-shock therapy', *Business Horizons* May–June: 6–18.

Goold, M. (1996) 'Design, planning and strategy: extra time' *California Management Review* 38 (4): 100–3.

Goold, M. and Campbell, A. (1987) *Strategies and Styles*, Oxford: Blackwell.

Gordon, C: (1988) 'France', in C. Hardy, C. Cordon, I. Gow and C. Randlesome (eds) *Making Managers*, London: Pitman.

Gordon, D. M., Edwards, R. and Reich, M. (1982) *Segmented Work, Divided Workers*, Cambridge: Cambridge University Press.

Graham, E. M. (1990) 'Exchange of threat between multinational firms as an infinitely repeated non cooperative game', *International Trade Journal* 4 (3): 259–77.

—— (1991) 'Strategic management and transnational firm behaviour: a formal approach', in C. N. Pitelis and R. Sugden (eds) *The Nature of the Transnational Firm*, London: Routledge.

Granovetter, M. (1985) 'Economic action and social structure: the problem of embeddedness', *American Journal of Sociology* 91(3): 481–510.

Grant, R. M. (1998) *Contemporary Strategy Analysis*, Oxford: Blackwell.

—— (1991) 'The resource-based theory of competitive advantage: implications for strategy formulation', *California Management Review* 33 (3): 114–22.

Greenley, G. E. (1990) 'Does strategic planning improve company performance?', in D. Asch and C. Bowman (eds) *Readings in Strategic Management*, London: Macmillan.

Grinyer, P., Mayes D. and McKiernan, P. (1988) *Sharpbenders: The Secrets of Unleashing Corporate Potential*, Oxford: Blackwell.

Grundfest, J. A. (1990) 'The subordination of American capital', *Journal of Financial Economics* 27: 89–114.

Gupta, A. K. and Wilemon, D. (1990) 'Improving R&D/marketing relations: R&D's perspective', *R&D Management* 20 (4): 277–90.

—— (1991) 'Improving R&D/marketing relations in technology-based companies', *Journal of Marketing Management* 7: 25–45.

Hall, D. J. and Saias, M. A. (1980) 'Strategy follows structure!', *Strategic Management Journal* 1: 149–63.

Hall, R. C. and Hitch, C. J. (1939) 'Price theory and business behaviour', *Oxford Economic Papers* 2:12–45.

Hambrick, D. C. (1983) 'Some tests of the effectiveness and functional attributes of Miles and Snow's strategic types', *Academy of Management Journal* 26 (1): 5–26.

Hamel, G. (1991) 'Competition for competence and interpartner learning within international alliances', *Strategic Management Journal* 12: 83–103.

Hamel, G. and Prahalad, C. K. (1985) 'Do you really have a global strategy?', *Harvard Business Review* July–August: 139–49.

—— (1989) 'Strategic intent', *Harvard Business Review* May–June: 63–76.

—— (1994) *Competing for the Future*, Boston, MA: Harvard Business School Press.

Hamilton, G. C. and Biggart, N. W. (1988) 'Market, cultures and authority: a comparative analysis of management and organisation in the Far East', *American Journal of Sociology* 94, Supplement: 52–94.

Hampden-Turner, C. and Trompenaars, F. (1993) *The Seven Cultures of Capitalism*, New York: Doubleday.

Hannan, M. T. (1997) 'Inertia, density and the structure of organizational populations: entries in European automobile industries, 1886–1981', *Organization Studies* 18 (2): 192–228.

Hannan, M. T. and Freeman, J. (1988) *Organizational Ecology*, Cambridge, MA: Harvard University Press.

Hax, A. and Majluf, N. (1990) 'The use of the growth-share matrix in strategic planning', in R. Dyson (ed.) *Strategic Planning: Models and Analytical Techniques*, London: Wiley.

Hayes, R. H. (1985) 'Strategic planning – forward in reverse?', *Harvard Business Review* November–December: 111–19.

Hayes, R. H. and Abernathy, W. (1980) 'Managing our way to economic decline', *Harvard Business Review* July–August: 67–75.

Hayes, R. H. and Garvin, D. A. (1982) 'Managing as if tomorrow mattered', *Harvard Business Review* May–June: 71–9.

Henderson, B. D. (1989) 'The origin of strategy', *Harvard Business Review* November–December: 139–43.

Helweg, M. D. (2000) 'A rising sun?' *Foreign Affairs* 79 (4): 26–40.

Hendry, J. (1989) 'Barriers to excellence and the politics of innovation', *Journal of General Management* 15 (2): 20–31.

Hennart, J.-F. (1988) 'Upstream vertical integration in the aluminium and tin industries', *Journal of Economic Behavior and Organization* 9: 281–99.

—— (1991) 'The transaction cost theory of the multinational enterprise', in C. N. Pitelis and R. Sugden (eds) *The Nature of the Transnational Firm*, London: Routledge.

Hickson, D. J., Butler, R. J., Cray, D., Mallory, G. R. and Wilson, D. C. (1986) *Top Decisions: Strategic Decision-making in Organizations*, Oxford: Blackwell.

Hiromoto, T. (1988) 'Japanese management accounting', *Harvard Business Review* July–August: 22–6.

Hitt, M. A., Dacin, T. C., Tyler, B. B. and Park, D. (1997) 'Understanding the differences in Korean and US executives' strategic orientations', *Strategic Management Journal* 18 (2): 159–67.

Holl, P. (1977), 'Control type and the market for corporate control in large U.S. corporations', *Journal of Industrial Economics* 25 (4): 259–73.

Hollander, S. (1987) *Classical Economics*, Oxford: Blackwell.

Hollis, M. and Nell, E. J. (1975) *Rational Economic Man: A Philosophical Critique of Neo-Classical Economics*, Cambridge: Cambridge University Press.

Hoskin, K. (1990) 'Using history to understand theory: a reconceptualisation of the historical genesis of strategy', Paper presented to the European Institute for Advanced Studies in Management Workshop, Venice, October.

Hu, Y. S. (1992) 'Global or stateless corporations are national firms with international operations', *California Management Review* Winter: 115–26.

Hung, S.-C. and Whittington, R. (1997) 'Strategies and institutions: a pluralistic account of strategies in the Taiwanese computer industry', *Organization Studies* 18 (4): 551–67.

Imai, K. and Itami, H. (1984) 'Interpenetration of organization and market', *International Journal of Industrial Organization* 2: 285–310.

International Monetary Fund (2000) *International Financial Statistics*, June.

Ireland, R. D., Hitt, M. A., Bettis, R. A. and De Porras, D. A. (1987) 'Strategy formulation processes: differences in perceptions of strengths and weaknesses and environmental uncertainty by managerial level', *Strategic Management Journal* 8: 469–85.

Ishida, H. (1997) 'MBA education in Japan', *Journal of Management Development* 16 (2): 185–97.

Jackson, S. E. and Dutton, J. E. (1988) 'Discerning threats and opportunities', *Administrative Science Quarterly* 33: 370–87.

Jackson, T. (1998) *Inside Intel*, London: Harper Collins.

James, B. G. (1985) *Business Wargames*, Harmondsworth: Penguin.

Jarrell, G. and Poulsen, A. (1987) 'Shark repellants and stock prices: the effects of antitakeover amendments since 1980', *Journal of Financial Economics* 19: 127–68.

Jensen, M. C. (1989) 'Eclipse of the public corporation', *Harvard Business Review* September–October: 61–74.

Jensen, M. C. and Meckling, W. H. (1976) 'Theory of the firm: managerial behaviour, agency costs and ownership structure', *Journal of Financial Economics* 3: 305–60.

Jensen, M. C. and Ruback, R. S. (1983) 'The market for corporate control: the scientific evidence', *Journal of Financial Economics* 11: 5–50.

Johnson, G. (1987) *Strategic Change and the Management Process*, Oxford: Blackwell.

Johnson, G. and Scholes, K. (1999) *Exploring Corporate Strategy*, 5th edn, Englewood Cliffs, NJ: Prentice Hall.

Johnson, H. and Kaplan, R. (1987) *Relevance Lost: the Rise and Fall of Management Accounting*, Boston, MA: Harvard Business School.

Jones, A. M. and Hendry, C. (1992) *The Learning Organization: a Review of Literature and Practice*, London: The Human Resource Development Partnership.

Kanter, R. M. (1983) *The Change Masters*, New York: Simon & Schuster.

Karpik, L. (1978) 'Organisations, institutions and history', in L. Karpik (ed.) *Organisations and Environment*, London: Sage.

Kenney, M. and von Burg, U. (1999) 'Technology, entrepreneurship and path dependence: industrial clustering in Silicon Valley and Route 128', *Industrial and Corporate Change* 8 (1): 67–110.

Kets de Vries, M. F. R. (1988) 'Origins of charisma: ties that bind the leader and the led', in J. A. Conger and R. N. Kanungo (eds) *Charismatic Leadership*, London: Jossey Bass.

Keynes, J. M. (1936) *The General Theory of Employment, Interest and Money*, London: Macmillan.

Khanna, T. and Palepu, K. (1999) 'Policy shocks, market intermediaries and corporate strategy: the evolution of business groups in Chile and India', *Journal of Economics and Management Strategy* 8 (2): 271–310.

Kim, E. M. (1988) 'From dominance to symbiosis: state and chaebol in Korea', *Pacific Focus* 3 (2): 105–21.

Kimberley, J. R. and Zajac, E. J. (1988) 'Dynamics of C.E.O./board relationships', in D. C. Hambrick (ed.) *The Executive Effect*, Greenwich, CT: JAI Press.

Knickerbocker, F. T. (1973) *Oligopolistic Reaction and Multinational Enterprise*, Boston MA: Harvard University Press.

Knights, D. and Morgan, G. (1990) 'The concept of strategy in sociology: a note of dissent', *Sociology* 24 (3): 275–483.

—— (1991) 'Corporate strategy, organizations and subjectivity', *Organizational Studies* 12 (2): 251–73.

Kono, T. (1984) *Strategy and Structure of Japanese Enterprises*, London: Macmillan.

Kotter, J. P. (1990) 'What leaders really do', *Harvard Business Review* May–June: 103–11.

Langley, A. (1988) 'The role of formal strategic planning', *Long Range Planning* 21 (3): 40–50.

—— (1991) 'Formal analysis and strategic decision-making', *OMEGA* 19 (213): 79–99.

Laverty, K. J. (1997) 'Economic "short-termism": the debate, the unresolved issues and the implications for management research and practice', *Academy of Management Review* 21 (3): 825–60.

Lawriwsky, M. L. (1984) *Corporate Structure and Performance*, London: Croom Helm.

Lehrer, D. and Darbishire, O. (1999) 'Comparative managerial learning in Germany and Britain', in S. Quack, G. Morgan and R. Whitley (eds), *National Capitalisms, Global Competition and Economic Performance*, Amsterdam: John Benjamins.

Lengnick-Hall, C. and Wolff, J. (1999) 'Similarities and contradictions in the core logic of three strategy research themes', *Strategic Management Journal* 20 (12): 1109–32.

Leser, E. and Vidalie, A. (1991) 'Le Capital des 200 premières entreprises françaises', *Science et Vie Economique* 76, October: 46–57.

Levitt, T. (1960) 'Marketing myopia', *Harvard Business Review* July–August: 45–56.

Lindblom, C. E. (1959) 'The science of muddling through', *Public Administration Review* 19: 79–88.

Linzmayer, O. W. (1999) *Apple Confidential: the Real Story of Apple Computer Inc.*, San Francisco, CA: No Starch Press.

Lowendahl, B. and Revang, O. (1998) 'Challenges to existing strategy theory in a post-industrial society', *Strategic Management Journal* 19 (8): 755–74.

Mair, A. (1999) 'Learning from Honda', *Journal of Management Studies*, 36 (1): 25–46.

Marceau, J. (1989) *A Family Business? The Making of an International Business Elite*, Cambridge: Cambridge University Press.

March, J. G. (1976) 'The technology of foolishness', in J. Marsh and J. Olsen (eds) *Ambiguity and Choice in Organizations*, Bergen: Universitetsforlaget.

March, J. G. and Olsen, J. P. (1989) *Rediscovering Institutions*, New York: Free Press.

March, J. G. and Simon, H. A. (1958) *Organizations*, New York: Wiley.

Marris, R. (1964) *The Economic Theory of Managerial Capitalism*, London: Macmillan.

Markides, C. M. (2000) *All the Right Moves: a Guide to Crafting Breakthrough Strategy*, Boston, MA: Harvard Business School Press.

Marsh, P., Barwise, P., Thomas, K. and Wensley, R. (1988) *Managing Strategic Investment Decisions in Large Diversified Companies*, London: Centre for Business Strategy, London Business School.

Marx, K. (1954) *Capital: a Critique of Political Economy*, vol. l, Moscow: Progress Publishers.

Marx, K. and Engels, F. (1972) 'Manifesto of the Communist Party' (1848), in R. C. Tucker (ed.) *The Marx–Engels Reader*, New York: W. W. Norton.

Mayer, C. (1997) 'The city and corporate performance: condemned or exonerated?', *Cambridge Journal of Economics* 21 (2): 291–302.

Mayer, M. and Whittington, R. (1999) 'Strategy, structure and "systemness": national institutions and corporate changes in France, Germany and the UK, 1950–1993', *Organization Studies* 20(6): 933–60.

McCloskey, D. N. (1990) *If You're So Smart: the Narrative of Economic Expertise*, Chicago, IL: University of Chicago Press.

McGahan, A. and Porter, M. (1997) 'How much does industry matter, really?' *Strategic Management Journal* 18, Summer Special Issue: 15–30.

McGrath, R. G. (1999) 'Falling forward: real options reasoning and entrepreneurial failure', *Academy of Management Review* 24 (1): 13–30.

McKiernan, P. (1992) *Strategies of Growth: Maturity, Recovery and Internationalization*, London: Routledge.

McMillan, C. (1985) *The Japanese Industrial System*, Berlin: DeGruyter.

Meyer, J. W. and Rowan, B. (1977) 'Institutionalized organizations: formal structure as myth and ceremony', *American Journal of Sociology* 83 (2): 340–63.

Miles, R. E. and Snow, C. C. (1978) *Organization Strategy, Structure and Process*, New York: McGraw-Hill.

Miller, D. (1982) 'Evolution and revolution: a quantum view of structural change in organizations', *Journal of Management Studies* 19 (2): 131–51.

Miller, P. and O'Leary, T. (1990) 'Making accountancy practical', *Accounting, Organizations and Society* 15 (5): 479–98.

Mintzberg, H. (1978) 'Patterns in strategy formation', *Management Science* 24 (9): 934–48.

—— (1979) *The Structuring of Organizations*, Englewood Cliffs, NJ: Prentice Hall.

—— (1987) 'Crafting strategy', *Harvard Business Review* July–August: 65–75.

—— (1989) 'Strategy formation: schools of thought', in J. Fredrickson (ed.) *Perspectives on Strategic Management*, San Francisco, CA: Ballinger.

—— (1990) 'The design school: reconsidering the basic premises of strategic management', *Strategic Management Journal* 11: 171–95.

—— (1994) *The Rise and Fall of Strategic Planning*, New York: Free Press

—— (1996a) 'Learning 1, Planning 0', *California Management Review* 38 (4): 92–4.

—— (1996b) 'Musings on Management', *Harvard Business Review* July–August: 61–9.

Mintzberg, H., Ahlstrand, B. and Lampel, J. (1998) *Strategy Safari: a Guided Tour through the Wilds of Strategic Management*, London: Prentice Hall.

Mintzberg, H. and Waters, J. A. (1985) 'Of strategies, deliberate and emergent', *Strategic Management Journal* 6: 257–72.

—— (1990) 'Does decision get in the way?', *Organization Studies* 11(1): 1–5.

Mitchell, B. R. (1976) *European Historical Statistics*, London: Macmillan.

Miyake, M. and Thomsen, S. (2000) *Recent Trends in Foreign Investment*, Working Paper, Paris: OECD.

Moran, P. and Ghoshal, S. (1999) 'Markets, firms, and the process of economic development', *Academy of Management Review* 24 (3): 390–413.

Morck, R., Shleifer, A. and Vishnir, W. (1990) 'Do managerial objectives drive bad acquisitions?', *Journal of Finance* 45 (1): 31–48.

Morrison, A. and Wensley, R. (1991) 'Boxing up or boxed in? A short history of the Boston Consulting Group Share/Growth Matrix', *Journal of Marketing Management* 7: 105–29.

Mueller, D. C. (1985) 'Mergers and market share', *Review of Economics and Statistics* 47: 259–67.

—— (1987) *Profits in the Long Run*, Cambridge: Cambridge University Press.

Nadler, D. and Tushman, M. (1990) 'Beyond the charismatic leader: leadership and organizational change', *California Management Review* 31 (10): 77–97.

Nelson, R. R. (1992) 'Recent writings on competitiveness: boxing the compass', *California Management Review* Winter: 127–37.

Nelson, R. R. and Winter, S. G. (1982) *An Evolutionary Theory of Economic Change*, Cambridge, MA: Harvard University Press.

von Neumann, J. and Morgernstern, 0. (1944) *The Theory of Games and Economic Behaviour*, Princetown, NJ: Princeton University Press.

Noble, D. F. (1977) *America by Design*, Oxford: Oxford University Press.

Nöel, A. (1989) 'Strategic cores and management obsessions: discovering strategy formation through the daily activities of CEOs', *Strategic Management Journal* 10: 33–49.

Nonaka, I. (1988) 'Towards middle-up-down management', *Sloan Management Review* Spring: 918.

Nonaka, I. and Takeuchi, H. (1995) *The Knowledge-Creating Company: How Japanese Companies Create the Dynamics of Innovation*, New York: Oxford University Press.

Nonaka, I., Toyama, R. and Konno, N. (2000) 'SECI, *Ba* and leadership: a unified model of dynamic knowledge creation', *Long Range Planning* 33 (1): 5–34.

Norburn, D. and Grinyer, P. (1973–4) 'Directors without direction', *Journal of General Management* l (2): 37–48.

Nystrom, P. and Starbuck, W. H. (1984) 'To avoid organizational crises, unlearn', *Organizational Dynamics* Spring: 53–65.

Oakes, L., Townley, B. and Cooper, D. (1998) 'Business planning as pedagogy: language and control in a changing institutional field', *Administrative Science Quarterly* 43 (2): 257–92.

Okimoto, D. I. (1989) *Between MITI and the Market*, Stanford, CA: Stanford University Press.

Pascale, R. T. (1982) 'Our curious addiction to corporate grand strategy', *Fortune* 25 January: 115–16.

—— (1984) 'Perspectives on strategy: the real story behind Honda's success', *California Management Review* 24 (3): 47–72.

—— (1991) *Managing on the Edge*, New York: Simon & Schuster.

—— (1996) 'The Honda effect', *California Management Review* 38 (4): 80–91.

—— (1999) 'Surfing the edge of chaos', *Sloan Management Review* Spring: 83–92.

Pelikan, P. (1989) 'Evolution, economic competence and the market for corporate control', *Journal of Economic Behaviour and Organization* 12: 279–303.

Penrose, E. T. (1952) 'Biological analogies in the theory of the firm', *American Economic Review* 42 (5): 804–19.

Perrow, C. (1981) 'Markets, hierarchies and hegemony', in A. H. Van de Ven and W. F. Joyce (eds) *Perspectives on Organization Design and Behavior*, New York: Wiley.

Peters, T. (1992) *Liberation Management*, London: Macmillan.

Petroni, G. (1983) 'The strategic management of R&D', *Long Range Planning* 16 (2): 51–64.

Pettigrew, A. M. (1973) *The Politics of Organizational Decision-Making*, London: Tavistock.

—— (1985) *The Awakening Giant: Continuity and Change in ICI*, Oxford: Blackwell.

—— (1990) 'Studying strategic choice and change', *Organization Studies* 11(1): 6–11.

Pettigrew, A. and Fenton, E. (2000) *The Innovating Organization*, London: Sage.

Pettigrew, A. and Whipp, R. (1991) *Managing Change for Competitive Success*, Oxford: Blackwell.

Pinch, S. and Henry, N. (1999) 'Paul Krugman's geographical economics, industrial clustering and the British motor sport industry', *Regional Studies* 33 (9): 815–27.

Piore, M. J. and Sabel, C. F. (1984) *The Second Industrial Divide*, New York: Basic Books.

Porac, J., Thomas, H. and Baden-Fuller, C. (1989) 'Competitive groups as cognitive communities: the case of Scottish knitwear manufacturers', *Journal of Management Studies* 26 (4): 397–416.

Porter, M. E. (1980) *Competitive Strategy: Techniques for Analysing Industries and Firms*, New York: Free Press and Macmillan.

—— (1985) *Competitive Advantage: Creating and Sustaining Superior Performance*, New York: Free Press.

—— (1990) *The Competitive Advantage of Nations*, New York, Free Press.

—— (1996) 'What is strategy?', *Harvard Business Review* November–December: 61–78.

—— (1998) 'Location, clusters and the "new" microeconomics of competition', *Business Economics* 33 (1) 7–13.

Quinn, J. B. (1980) *Strategies for Change: Logical Incrementalism*, Homewood, IL: Richard D. Irwin.

—— (1985) 'The management of innovation: controlled chaos', *Harvard Business Review* May–June: 73–84.

—— (1991) 'Polaroid corporation', in H. Mintzberg and J. B. Quinn (eds) *The Strategy Process: Concepts, Contexts, Cases*, 2nd edn, Englewood Cliffs, NJ: Prentice Hall.

Ramanujam, V. and Varadarajam, P. (1989) 'Research on corporate diversification', *Strategic Management Journal* 10: 523–51.

Rappaport, A. (1990) 'The staying power of the public corporation', *Harvard Business Review* January–February: 96–104.

Ravenscraft, D. and Scherer, F. (1987) *Mergers, Sell-Offs and Economic Efficiency*, Washington, DC: Brookings Institution.

Reader, W. J. (1975) *Imperial Chemical Industries: a History*, vol. 2, *The First Quarter Century, 1926–1952*, London: Oxford University Press.

Reading, J. G. (1990) *The Spirit of Chinese Capitalism*, New York: DeGruyter.

Reid, D. M. and Schlegelmilch, B. B. (1990) 'Planning and control in the UK and West Germany: the mechanical engineering industry', *Marketing Intelligence and Planning* 8 (4): 30–8.

Rugman, A. (1980) 'Internalization as a general theory of foreign direct investment', *Weltwirtschaftliches Archiv* 116: 365–79.

Rumelt, R. (1991) 'How much does industry matter?' *Strategic Management Journal* 12 (3): 167–85.

Rumelt, R. (1996) 'The many faces of Honda', *California Management Review* 38 (4): 103–11.

Rumelt, R. P., Schendel, D. and Teece, D. J. (1991) 'Strategic management and economics', *Strategic Management Journal* 12: 5–29.

Sadanori, A. (1999) 'How Matsushita Electric and Sony manage global R&D', *Research Technology Management* 42 (2): 41–52.

Sadler, P. (1989) 'A training scandal?', in K. Sisson (ed.) *Personnel Management in Britain*, Oxford: Blackwell.

Sampler, J. (1998) 'Redefining industry structure for the information age', *Strategic Management Journal* 19 (4): 343–56.

Sanchez, R. and Sudharshan, D. (1992) 'Real-time market research: learning by doing in the development of new products', in C. Karlsson (ed.) *Proceedings of the International Product Development Conference*, Brussels: European Institute for Advanced Studies in Management.

Saviotti, P. and Metcalfe, J. (1991) *Evolutionary Theories and Technological Change*, Chur: Harwood.

Saxenian, A. (1999) 'Comment on Kenney and von Burg: technology, entrepreneurship and path dependence: industrial clustering in Silicon Valley and Route 128, *Industrial and Corporate Change* 8 (1): 105–110.

Scarborough, H. H. and Corbett, J. M. (1992) *Technology and Organisation: Power, Meaning and Design*, London: Routledge.

Scarpetta, S., Bassanini, A., Pilat, D. and Schreyer, P. (2000) 'Economic growth in the OECD area: recent trends at the aggregate and sectoral level', *Economics Department Working Paper No. 248*, Paris: Organisation for Economic Co-operation and Development.

Schapiro, C. and Varian, H. (1999) 'The Art of Standard Wars', *California Management Review* 41 (2): 8–32.

Schumpeter, J. A. (1934) *The Theory of Economic Development*, Cambridge, MA: Harvard University Press.

Schwartz, E. I. (1999) *Digital Darwinism*, London: Penguin.

Scott, J. (1990) 'Corporate control and corporate rule', *British Journal of Sociology* 41(3): 351–73.

—— (1991) 'A comparative assessment: networks of corporate power', *Annual Review of Sociology* 17: 181–203.

—— (1997) *Corporate Business and Capitalist Classes*, Oxford: Oxford University Press.

Senge, P. M. (1990) 'The leader's new work: building learning organizations', *Sloan Management Review* Fall: 7–22.

Servan-Schreiber, J. (1969) *The American Challenge*, London: Penguin.

Sexty, R. W. (1998) 'Teaching business ethics in transitional economies', *Journal of Business Ethics* 17 (12): 1311–17.

Shaiken, H. (1985) *Work Transformed*, New York: Holt, Rinehart & Winston.

Sheng, A. (1999) 'Asia's governance challenge', *Corporate Board* March–April: 20–4.

Shrivastava, P. (1986) 'Is strategic management ideological?', *Journal of Management* 12 (3): 363–77.

Simmonds, K. (1986) 'Marketing as innovation: the eighth paradigm', *Journal of Management Studies* 23 (5): 479–500.

Slatter, S. (1984) *Corporate Recovery*, Harmondsworth: Penguin.

Sloan, A. P. (1963) *My Years with General Motors*, London: Sedgewick & Jackson.

Smith, M. (1996) 'Shareholder activism by institutional investors: evidence from CalPERS', *Journal of Finance* 51, 1: 227–52.

Sorenson, O. (2000) 'Letting the market work for you: an evolutionary perspective on product strategy', *Strategic Management Journal* 21 (5): 577–92.

Spender, J.-C. (1989) *Industrial Recipes*, Oxford: Blackwell.

Stallings, S. (1999) 'A visible hand', *Harvard International Review* 21 (3): 14–15.

Starkey, K. and Whittington, R. (1999) 'Postmodernism and Strategy', Unpublished working paper, Nottingham University Business School.

Stearns, L. and Allen, K. (1996) 'Economic behavior in institutional environments: the corporate merger wave of the 1980s', *American Sociological Review* 61: 699–718.

Stiglitz, J. E. (1985) 'Credit markets and the control of capital', *Journal of Money, Credit and Banking* 17 (2): 133–52.

Storey, J. and Sisson, K. (1990) 'Limits to transformation: human resource management in the British context', *Industrial Relations Journal*: 60–5.

Swedberg, R., Himmelstrand, W. and Brulin, G. (1987) 'The paradigm of economic sociology', *Theory and Society* 16 (2): 169–213.

Tate, P. (1991) 'Happy birth to a trend-setter', *Financial Times* 16 July.

Teece, D. J. (1982) 'Towards an economic theory of the multi-product firm', *Journal of Economic Behaviour and Organization* 3: 39–63.

—— (1986) 'Transaction cost economics and the multinational enterprise', *Journal of Economic and Business Organization* 7: 21–45.

Teece, D., Pisano, G. and Shuen, A. (1997) 'Dynamic capabilities and strategic management', *Strategic Management Journal* 18 (7): 509–34.

Temin, P. (1999) 'The stability of the American business elite', *Industrial and Corporate Change* 8 (2): 189–209.

Thomsen, S. and Pedersen, T. (2000) 'Ownership structure and performance in the largest European companies', *Strategic Management Journal* 21 (6): 689–705.

Tsang, E. (1998) 'Can *Guanxi* be a source of sustained competitive advantage for doing business in China?', *Academy of Management Executive* 12 (2): 64–73.

Tsoukas, T. (1996) 'The firm as a distributed knowledge system: a constructionist approach', *Strategic Management Journal* 17, Winter Special Issue: 11–26.

Useem, M. (1984) *The Inner Circle*, New York: Oxford University Press.

Volberda, H. (1998) *Building the Flexible Firm*, Oxford: Oxford University Press.

Walker, R. (1988) 'The geographical organization of production systems', *Environment and Planning D: Society and Space* 6: 377–408.

Weick, K. E. (1990) 'Cartographic myths in organizations', in A. Huff (ed.) *Mapping Strategic Thought*, London: Wiley.

Wensley, R. (1981) 'Strategic marketing: betas, boxes or basics', *Journal of Marketing* 45: 173–82.

Westley, F. and Mintzberg, H. (1989) 'Visionary leadership and strategic management', *Strategic Management Journal* 10: 17–32.

Westwood, R. (1997) 'Harmony and patriarchy: the cultural basis for paternalistic headship amongst the overseas Chinese', *Organization Studies* 18 (3): 445–80.

Whipp, R., Rosenfeld, R. and Pettigrew, P. (1989) 'Culture and competitiveness: evidence from two mature UK industries', *Journal of Management Studies* 26 (6): 561–85.

Whitley, R. D. (1990) 'East Asian entrepreneurial structures and the comparative analysis of forms of business organization', *Organization Studies* 11 (1): 47–74.

—— (1991) 'The social construction of business systems in East Asia', *Organization Studies* 12 (1): 1–28.

—— (1999) *Divergent Capitalisms*, Oxford: Oxford University Press

Whittington, R. (1988) 'Environmental structure and theories of strategic choice', *Journal of Management Studies* 25 (6): 521–36.

—— (1989) *Corporate Strategies in Recession and Recovery: Social Structures and Strategic Choice*, London: Unwin Hyman.

—— (1990) 'Social structures and resistance to strategic change: British manufacturers in the 1980s', *British Journal of Management* 1: 201–13.

—— (1991a) 'Changing control strategies in industrial R&D', *R&D Management* 21 (1): 43–53.

—— (1991b) 'Recession strategies and top management change', *Journal of General Management* 16 (3): 11–28.

—— (1992) 'Putting Giddens into action: social systems and managerial agency', *Journal of Management Studies* 29 (6): 693–712.

—— (1996) 'Strategy as practice', *Long Range Planning* October: 731–5.

Whittington, R. and Mayer, M. (2001) *The European Corporation: Strategy, Structure and Social Science*, Oxford: Oxford University Press.

Whittington, R., Pettigrew, A., Peck, S., Fenton, E. and Conyon, M. (1999) 'Change and complementarities in the new competitive landscape: a European panel study, 1992–1996', *Organization Science* 10 (5): 583–600.

Whittington, R. and Whipp, R. (1992) 'Professional ideology and marketing implementation', *European Journal of Marketing* 26 (1): 52–63.

Wilks, S. (1990) 'The embodiment of industrial culture in bureaucracy and management', in S. Clegg and S. G. Redding (eds) *Capitalism in Contrasting Cultures*, Berlin: DeGruyter.

Williams, K., Haslam, C. and Williams, J. (1991a) 'Management accounting: the Western problematic against the Japanese application', 9th Annual Conference on the Labour Process, University of Manchester Institute of Science and Technology.

Williams, K., Mitsui, I. and Haslam, C. (1991b) 'How far from Japan? A case study of Japanese press shop practice and management calculation', *Critical Perspectives on Accounting* 2: 145–69.

Williams, P. (1991) 'Time and the city: short termism in the UK, myth or reality?', *National Westminster Bank Quarterly Review* August: 31–8.

Williamson, O. E. (1967) *The Economics of Discretionary Behaviour*, Chicago, IL: Markham.

—— (1975) *Markets and Hierarchies: Analysis and Antitrust Implications*, New York: Free Press.

—— (1985) *The Economic Institutions of Capitalism*, New York: Free Press.

—— (1988) 'The economics and sociology of organizing: promoting a dialogue', in G. Farkas and P. England (eds) *Industries, Firms and Jobs*, New York: Plenum.

—— (1991) 'Strategizing, economizing and economic organization', *Strategic Management Journal* 12: 75–94.

—— (1999) 'Strategy research: governance and competence perspectives', *Strategic Management Journal* 20 (12): 1087–108.

Wilson, D. C. (1992) *A Strategy of Change: Concepts and Controversies in the Management of Change*, London: Routledge.

Wilson, I. (1990) 'The state of strategic planning: what went wrong? what goes right?', *Technological Forecasting and Social Change* 37: 103–10.

Yamazaki, H. (1988) 'The development of large enterprises in Japan (1929–1984)', *Japanese Business History Yearbook* 5:12–53.

Yatsko, P. (1998) 'The bigger, the better', *Far Eastern Economic Review* 161 (21): 10–14.

Yoshikawa, T., Innes, J. and Mitchell, F. (1995) 'A Japanese case study of financial control analysis', *Management Accounting Review* 6: 415–32.

Yu, C.-M. and Ito, K. (1989) 'Oligopolistic reaction and foreign direct investment: the case of the US tire and textiles industries', *Journal of International Business Studies* 20: 449–60.

Yui, T. (1988) 'Development, organisation and business strategy of industrial enterprises in Japan', *Japanese Business History Yearbook* 5: 56–78.

Zack, M. (1999) 'Developing a knowledge strategy', *California Management Review* 41 (3): 125–46.

I ndex

accountancy and decision-making
63–71
acquisitions and mergers 82–9
adaptive approach 22–4, 108
agency approach 109, 110
Alchian, A.A. 16, 19
Aldrich, H.E. 19
Amazon.com 67
Amtrak 81
Anglo-Saxon model 5, 29, 31, 33;
    acquisitions/mergers 82, 86–7;
    decision-making 65; growth
    strategies 78; leadership 46, 50;
    national policy consequences
    126
Ansoff, Igor 13
Aoki, M. 33
Apple Computers 28, 42, 113–14
Argyris, C. 9–10, 112, 118
Armstrong, P. 50–1
Asian crisis 127–8
Australia 127

banking 31, 32, 125–6
bargaining process 22
Barnard, Chester 29, 46
Barwise, P. 59
Bauer, M. and Bertin-Mourot, B.
    52, 53
Bayer 41
Berezovsky, Boris 123
Berners-Lee, Tim 79
Birds Eye 90
Borsch, Fred 66
Bosch, Robert 41

Boston Boxes 71
Boston Consulting Group (BCG)
    66, 71
bounded rationality 22, 100
Boyacigiller, N. and Adler, N. 28
Bracker, J. 13
Brownlie, D.T. 79
Brunsson, N. 62, 63
business schools 54–5, 70–1,
    121–2

Cadbury's 90
CalPERS effect 109
Canada 69, 74
Canon 64, 81
capitalism 32
Carlzon, Jan 42, 55
Carnegie School 21–2
Caterpillar 78
Celera Genomics 76
CERN 79–80
Chandler, A.D. 11, 12–13, 41, 48,
    50, 52, 83, 84, 91, 100, 102, 103,
    107, 108
change 108–16
chaos 24
China 96
Chung, Mong-koo 44
Classical approach 10, 11–16,
    28–9, 30, 37–8, 39; decision-
    making 57, 58, 72; fallacies of
    68; growth strategies 73, 74–5,
    82, 84, 88–9, 95, 96–7;
    leadership 45, 55; managerial
    consequences 118, 119;